A DEVOTIONAL

HE.
WE.
THEY.

THE LIFE-ALTERING FORMULA
OF THE LORD'S PRAYER

BY DWAYNE MOORE

A Next Level Worship Resource
nextlevelworship.com

ISBN 978-1-63877-582-9 (softcover)
ISBN 978-1-63877-584-3 (ebook)

Edited by Sandy Bayens
Designed by the NLW team

Special thanks to Sandy Bayens for sharing her expertise as an editor and her passion for prayer through this project. She is a God-send and blessing to our NLW team.

Unless otherwise noted, Scripture passages are from the Holy Bible, New International Version®, NIV® Copyright © 1973, 1978, 1984, 2011 by Biblica, Inc.® Used by permission. All rights reserved worldwide.

Cover image from Canva.com. Used by permission.

For requests to translate this material into other languages or to use extended quotes from it, please contact office@nextlevelworship.com.

To schedule Dwayne or one of our NLW team members for your church or conference, contact bookings@nextlevelworship.com.

For companion resources for this study and to connect with others who love prayer and worship, go to www.prayermodel.com.

Next Level Worship resources work!
Our team at Next Level Worship International is committed to excellent discipleship resources that help Christians grow as whole-life worshipers. We guarantee this resource can help you understand and experience deeper worship and communion with the Father.

For more resources by Dwayne Moore and our NLW team, please visit our website.

Join our global community of church leaders, worship teams & worshipers!
More info at nextlevelworship.com

CONTENTS

To my wife, Sonia, who has always modeled
a lifestyle of true worship and prayer

WHAT OTHERS ARE SAYING

HE. WE. THEY. is just so rich. When the disciples said, "Lord, teach us to pray," Jesus used the Model Prayer to teach the disciples to pray. And in a real sense, Dwayne used the Prayer Model to help teach me to pray. Some things I'd never even *thought* of before. For instance, Dwayne brings out that this is the first prayer in the Bible to address God as Father. What a mind-blowing shift that is! I'd never thought of that. For 5 weeks *HE. WE. THEY.* was what I used for my quiet time. I've done Bible studies from time to time. But if they don't engage me, then I move on to something else. *HE. WE. THEY.* grabbed me from the get-go. I marked the book up, marked the Bible up, and they both marked me up! I can't wait to take my whole congregation through *HE. WE. THEY!*

Dr. Randy Norris, founding pastor, The Station Church, Hoover, AL

HE. WE. THEY. is the best book Dwayne has written. It is theologically sound. It is theologically deep. Yet, it is written in such a way that the average church member interacts with it very easily. Dwayne has taken hard concepts and made them easy for the average person to understand, even someone who's not a believer who picks up the book. Unbelievers also understand the need to pray, and I think it can draw them evangelistically. We used *HE. WE. THEY.* church-wide at First Baptist Lexington. It is tailor-made for a church-wide emphasis. It wasn't a theological treatise on prayer. It actually draws you to communicate with God and for God to communicate with you. And here is the genius of the writing: When you get to the end of the daily lessons, it includes practical actions to take. Those actions become habits that are formed in your prayer life that you carry with you going forward.

Dr. Clay Hallmark, pastor of First Baptist Church Lexington, TN & 2022 President of the Tennessee Baptist State Convention

If you find a study on prayer that helps you adore God and love him more, read it. If you discover one that leads you to abide in Christ for your needs, enjoy it. But if you happen to come across a book on prayer that also prompts you to love others and attend to their needs, then cherish it, for you have discovered a rare jewel. *HE. WE. THEY. The Life-Altering Formula of the Lord's Prayer* is a rare find that can help transform how you approach prayer and forever deepen how you relate to God and others.

Charles Billingsley, worship artist & author

As a Christian, I thought, "I know the Model Prayer. I've done plenty of studies on that. I've got that down." But the great thing about *HE. WE. THEY.* is it breaks down every single word to help you think deeply about the rich and meaningful words within the Model Prayer. It's really overwhelming. This book absolutely made a difference in my prayer life.

Krystal Barker, church member & Sunday School teacher

HE. WE. THEY. is among the best stuff Dwayne has written. It is sure to impact many churches and transform many believers into powerful, life-long prayer warriors. What a gift to the Body of Christ!

Dr. Scott Dawson, evangelist & author

Captivating. Compelling. Brilliant. Moving. Worshipful. Deep. Model. Meaningful. Life-changing–these are just a few of the words that come to mind when I think of my friend Dwayne Moore, his ministry, and his book, *HE. WE. THEY.* I highly recommend you incorporate this new work into your devotional life.

Greg Atkinson, Founder of Worship Impressions & the First Impressions Conference

The most interesting part about this book is the elements of he-we-they as a "prayer model." I'd never heard it approached like that. I've done wonderful studies on prayer by such men as E.M. Bounds and Homer Lindsay. Yet, none have been nearly as good as *HE. WE. THEY.*

Glenn Sorensen, deacon & small group leader

Dwayne's book *HE. WE. THEY.* is timely, well-written, and needed for this time in the life of our culture and of the Church.

Dr. Michael Catt, longtime pastor of Sherwood Baptist Church in GA

INTRODUCTION

Three simple words: HE. WE. THEY. Yet in them lie the "secret" to powerful, effective, and deeply intimate prayer with our heavenly Father. I invite you on a journey, a journey to uncover the meaning and purpose behind the Lord's Prayer. Together, we can discover how Jesus himself intends for us to pray.

Throughout this study you will see the Model Prayer referred to as a "prayer model." That's because it can serve as a model for our prayers. Over the next five weeks, we'll discover why the Model Prayer is meant for more than just funerals and weddings. As beautiful as it is to recite with congregations, it is of much more value than something to be used only in church services. We need to learn to apply the Model Prayer in our everyday lives.

As with every resource we offer at NLW International, the underlying purpose of this book is to help people become whole-life worshipers. It is not necessarily our goal, mind you, for Christians to call themselves "worshipers." That might seem surprising, considering the name of our ministry is *Next Level Worship*. However, while we are not overly concerned with whether folks *see* themselves as worshipers, it is very important to us (and to God) that they *be* lifestyle worshipers.

The idea of biblical worship is that we give ourselves completely over to the Lord. He should be the most important person in our life. We should give worship to him above anything else. Such devotion has been called "loving God," "honoring God," "worshiping God." It doesn't really matter so much what we call it. What matters is that we *do* it.

The Model Prayer in Matthew 6 and Luke 11 is a proven tool to help us become true worshipers of God. This famous prayer can help shape our minds and hearts to honor God with everything we are. That's a thrilling result we can see from praying the pattern of HE, WE, THEY consistently!

How It Works

This is a "devotional study," which means the daily lessons are designed to provide the reader with both information and inspiration. Whenever you see this symbol ⚓ it's your opportunity to look up Scripture and interact with the study in some way. Be sure to take time to read the Scripture passages and respond to any reflection questions you may be asked.

Each week of the study has five daily lessons. The lessons can take 20 minutes or longer to complete, depending on how much time you choose to meditate and linger. I encourage you not to rush through the lessons and not to read ahead, since they build on each other. There is much to gain from each lesson. Give yourself time to absorb each day's truths before moving on to the next one. Read through each lesson carefully during your quiet time, and be sure to look up each Bible passage. This is vital for your growth and understanding. Then, throughout the day, allow your mind and heart to digest what you have learned.

At the end of each lesson, there's a section for "Praying the Prayer" and "Living the Prayer." These are both important to help you build a daily pattern of prayer. Please take the needed time to complete this section and journal your thoughts.

Small Groups & Churches

Group discussion questions are located at the end of each week's lessons. Want to take your entire church through this material as a prayer emphasis? Pastor's sermon outlines, small group lessons, teaching videos and other resources are available at *www.prayermodel.com*.

I'm Going Too!

I need this expedition of learning and discovery as much as anyone. I'm excited at what our Lord can show to us as we journey through this study together. I plan to share what I'm learning with a small circle of friends who will pray with me and encourage me to keep going in the lessons. I hope you will do the same. Be sure to go to *prayermodel.com* and share your discoveries with us through the study.

I don't think anyone ever quite "graduates" from the school of prayer, but I sure hope to make some serious strides toward communing better with my Savior and living a more abundant life. Hope you'll join me and finish this worthwhile journey for his glory!

Dwayne Moore

WEEK 1 PATTERNED PRAYER

Our Father which art in heaven, Hallowed be thy name. Thy kingdom come. Thy will be done in earth, as it is in heaven. Give us this day our daily bread. And forgive us our debts, as we forgive our debtors. And lead us not into temptation, but deliver us from evil: For thine is the kingdom, and the power, and the glory, for ever. Amen.
Matthew 6:9b-13 KJV

DAY 1 *WHY THE MODEL PRAYER?*

In his book *With Christ In the School of Prayer*, Andrew Murray describes the Model Prayer as "a form of prayer in which there breathe the freshness and fullness of the Eternal Life. So simple that the child can lisp it, so divinely rich that it comprehends all that God can give. A form of prayer that becomes the model and inspiration of all other prayer, and yet always draws us back to itself as the deepest utterance of our souls before our God."[1]

The ancient Christian author and apologist Tertullian once called the Lord's Prayer "an abridgment of the entire Gospel."[2]

Martin Luther said, "Whatever needs are in the world, they are included in the Lord's Prayer. And all the prayers in the Psalms and all the prayers which could ever be devised are in the Lord's Prayer."[3]

Author and seminary president Dr. Albert Mohler wrote this about the Lord's Prayer: "It stands at the very center of the Sermon on the Mount and so should stand at the very center of our lives as Christ's followers. For this and many other reasons, Christians need to regularly revisit the rich theology of the Lord's Prayer."[4]

Yes, but Why?

Even with all the accolades surrounding the Lord's Prayer, few seem to sufficiently explain why—really why—this particular prayer gets so much attention. Sure, we know Jesus said that we should pray this prayer. And the very fact that Jesus uttered it must mean it holds great significance. But why? Many Christians seem ready to dutifully recite the words of the prayer when called upon; yet honestly, many of us don't know why it matters or what it means.

Perhaps you see the Model Prayer the way some see the Mona Lisa. The Mona Lisa is a masterpiece, painted by Leonardo da Vinci, and remains the most popular in the Louvre Museum in Paris. But do you know why? Most people have heard of the Mona Lisa. They can even tell you something about the lady in the painting—her smile, her folded hands, the landscape around her. Yet many don't understand why it is considered the apex of art throughout the world. They have no idea why it deserves such an iconic status. I read about a man who sat and stared at the Mona Lisa for an entire day. His conclusion was that once someone actually *sees* the painting and studies its contours up close, he or she will realize it truly is one of the greatest masterpieces ever conceived.

Similarly, it could be of great benefit to us if we took time to "stare" at the Lord's Prayer and study it up close. Perhaps we, too, would begin to see it as the masterpiece it is.

♪ Please read Luke 11:1-4 from your Bible. Now read it again, but this time, imagine yourself in the scene, hearing Jesus pray. How might you have felt? Would you have wanted to approach him like the disciple did? Would you have asked, "Teach me to pray"? What about the prayer he instructed his disciples to pray? Would his words have inspired and encouraged you, or might they have caused you to have more questions and confusion?

The scene in Luke 11 may not have been the first time Jesus instructed the disciples on how to pray. Nonetheless, they still did not quite get it. In verse 1, a disciple heard Jesus praying and said, "Lord, teach us to pray." Notice that he was apparently the only one who stepped up and asked. Perhaps not all of Jesus' disciples had a strong desire to learn more about prayer. Some may have thought they already knew enough about it. After all, the Jews had been praying to God for hundreds of years, and the Pharisees and religious leaders may have trained some of the disciples as children about prayer. Therefore, they may have felt they already knew how to pray.

Fortunately, there was at least one person listening to Jesus pray who yearned to grow more in his communion with God. He didn't think he'd arrived or graduated from the school of prayer. It is likely that disciple had seen the power of Jesus' prayers and sensed the closeness he had with his Father, and he wanted to experience that kind of intimate prayer in his own life.

Some people might see this study and think, "There are hundreds of books about the Lord's Prayer, and thousands of sermons have been preached on it. So why write another study on the Model Prayer? Hasn't enough been written and said already? Can't we just dispense with more study on prayer?"

No, actually we cannot, because some still want and need to be taught better how to pray. We need to understand how the Model Prayer can shape our hearts for worship. As we go through this study together, I believe we will discover a new perspective on prayer that will deepen our communion with God and increase the effectiveness of our prayers and worship.

Teach Us to Pray

We should stop and ask ourselves: Do we understand all we need to about prayer? Are we satisfied with our level of communion with the Father? Am I content with my worship of God? If the answer in your heart to these questions is yes, then you may not need to go through this study. This study is for people who don't believe they know enough about prayer and who want to pray more effectively.

Look closely at the words "Lord, teach us to pray" in verse 1. To say to Jesus "Lord, teach us" implies the disciple saw Jesus as someone who could instruct them, someone who had knowledge and authority to teach them. The request to "teach us" reveals submission. It requires humility. It means "What you tell me, I will try to understand; what you have to teach me I'm not going to assume I already know; I am here to be taught by you." That's the heart of a student, and that's how we must approach any study on prayer.

"Lord, teach us *to pray*." That's a very specific request. Notice the disciple didn't say, "Lord, teach us to preach," or "Teach us to teach." He said, "Lord, teach us to *pray*." If we truly understood what it could cost to pray the way he showed us, would we still ask Jesus to instruct us on prayer? We would have the responsibility to apply what he taught us. We would no longer be able to plead innocence for our lack of understanding. Once Jesus shows us deeper truths about prayer, we'll be held accountable for what we've learned.

If we sincerely want to grow in our prayer lives, we need to become students of the Model Prayer. It's only a few words in length; yet nestled within its phrases is the essence of what prayer should be for all of us. If we are to be a people of prayer, then honestly, our only choice is to keep learning and growing in prayer.

Commands to pray are throughout God's word. The question isn't, "Should I know about prayer?" And it certainly isn't "Should I pray?" The answer to those queries will always be a resounding "Yes!" The real question for each of us is this: "Do I know *enough* about prayer, or is there more I need to learn?" Until you and I hunger and thirst after righteousness, until we are willing to quiet our preconceived notions about prayer and worship and truly *listen* to the Lord like one being taught, we are not ready to enter the intensive school of prayer. We are not yet prepared to explore the rich and wonderful depths of our Savior's standard on prayer.

Praying the Prayer

At the end of each lesson, you will be asked to respond through journaling, or prayer, or a time of praise. Today, please go back and reread the prayer Jesus told his disciples to pray in Luke 11:2-4. Pretend this is your first time to ever hear it. Pray it aloud to God now. Make it your sincere prayer to him.

Plan now to recite the Lord's Prayer at least three different times throughout your day. Think about ways you can apply the prayer today and live it out at home and at work or school.

Living the Prayer

Journal a prayer of your own below, asking the Lord to help you learn and apply the Model Prayer to your life in these coming days and weeks.

God please help me open my heart & mind to you so I can better grasp what powerful prayer is. Give me the hindsight to grasp concepts that I may not fully understand currently. Teach me Lord as I am all yours.

amen—

DAY 2: *WHAT PRAYER IS AND ISN'T*

I want you to think back to the first time you prayed. Do you remember it? Perhaps your first prayer was when you prayed to trust Christ as your Savior, or maybe it was when you were in trouble about something and you uttered a prayer out of desperation. It could be that your first time to pray was with a group at your school or at church when you were growing up. Or maybe you were like me, just a wee child when you first talked with God.

One day when I was around 4 years of age, I misplaced my favorite blanket and couldn't find it anywhere in the house. I didn't want to admit to my mom that I'd lost it because I was afraid she might get upset with me. So the only thing I knew to do was pray. I don't recall exactly what I said in my first praying adventure, but I do vividly recall the image that immediately popped into my head when I prayed. In my mind I could clearly see where my blue blanket was hiding. I went to the place I believed it was, and sure enough, it was there, inside the clothes hamper, right where I'd imagined it to be.

Mere coincidence, you say? I don't think so, for in that moment a little seed of faith planted itself deep inside my tender heart. That was my first encounter with the living God, and he came through for me and answered my simple but important-to-a-four-year-old request!

What a privilege prayer is! In fact, I can't imagine life without prayer, can you? Matthew Henry writes, "You may as soon find a living man that does not breathe, as a living Christian that does not pray."[5] Almost everyone prays at some time to someone—even people who aren't followers of Jesus. In fact, surveys indicate that one in five unbelievers prays every day.[6]

Prayer is a part of every major world religion. It's one of the most ancient expressions of worship. In Islam, the call of the muezzin summons faithful Muslims to kneel in the direction of Mecca and pray to Allah with their heads to the floor. Buddhists practice a form of prayer that focuses on entering a state of cognitive tranquility.[7] Ancient Romans began their prayers with an invocation to a divinity. They had to be sure, though, that they didn't address the wrong god. So, to avoid this error, they had litanies of prayers for fifteen different gods and goddesses![8]

7

Christians pray too, but the major difference is that we pray to the Deity who is alive! Unlike members of other religions, we can communicate and commune with the one, true God. Anyone can attempt to pray, but unless someone is on the other end of that prayer listening and responding, one is not really praying. If you search online, you'll discover several places where prayer is defined as "talking to God." But that's not quite accurate with Christ-followers. It's more correct to say we talk *with* God. It's a conversation. As Max Lucado explains it, "We speak. He listens. He speaks. We listen. This is prayer in its purest form."[9]

Center of the Sermon

The Lord's Prayer is right in the middle of the Sermon on the Mount. Not only is it centrally located in the passage, its meaning is also at the heart of Jesus' teaching. Almost everything about his sermon seems to emanate from the Model Prayer.

- Near the beginning of his teaching, the Lord said we are to be salt and light on the earth. In the Model Prayer he prayed for God's kingdom to come to this earth, which is exactly what our "being salt and light" helps to accomplish.
- Jesus said in Matthew 6 we are to "Seek first the kingdom of God" (verse 33). Before he spoke those words, he had already sought the Father in the Lord's Prayer.
- In chapter 7 he told us to ask, seek and knock in prayer (verse 7). He set the example for making requests of God when he asked for daily bread and other provisions during the Model Prayer.
- Toward the close of his sermon, Jesus said to be careful of "wolves in sheep's clothing" (7:15). Moments before in his Model Prayer, Jesus prayed for protection from the evil one.

Please read Matthew chapter 6. Look for ways the Lord's Prayer supports the rest of the chapter. Now try to imagine the chapter *without* the Model Prayer. What differences could it have made if the prayer hadn't been included with Jesus' sermon?

What Prayer Is Not

Before Jesus demonstrated to his disciples how we should pray, he first warned of some things we *shouldn't* do. Matthew 6 starts with instructions from the Lord that are clear and to the point: "Beware of practicing your righteousness before other people in order to be seen by them, for then

8

you will have no reward from your Father who is in heaven" (ESV).

He went on to say that we shouldn't pray "like the hypocrites who lo to pray publicly on street corners and in the synagogues where everyone can see them" (verse 5 NLT). Furthermore, we shouldn't "babble on and on as people of other religions do. They think their prayers are answered merely by repeating their words again and again" (verse 7 NLT). Prayers that honor God don't need to be showy and they don't need to be lengthy mantras. God already knows our thoughts and sees our needs.

What Prayer Should Be

Humble.

Please read Luke 18:9-13. Why do you think Jesus chose this story to illustrate humility? Based on this passage, how important is humility in prayer, and why?

E.M. Bounds writes, "As a ship is made for the sea, so prayer is made for humility, and so humility is made for prayer."[10] Humility in prayer is vital because "God opposes the proud but favors the humble" (1 Peter 5:5b NLT).

In the Sermon on the Mount, Jesus told his disciples, "But when you pray, go away by yourself, shut the door behind you, and pray to your Father in private" (Matthew 6:6a NLT). Jesus knew that only people who are serious about prayer would hide themselves away where no one could see them or pat them on the back for praying. Jesus basically drew a line in the sand. He separated those who truly *want* to pray to God from those who may have ulterior motives for their prayers.

Simple.

It's been said, "Good things come in small packages," and nothing could be truer of the Model Prayer. Not even 70 words long, yet it sets the standard for all the prayers in God's Word and all prayers of the Christian faith.

The verses that embody the Lord's Prayer have to be some of the most astounding Scriptures in the entire Bible. I mean, think about it: Can you imagine sitting there around Jesus' feet that day, listening to him teach on prayer? The moment you hear him say, "Pray like this," what might cross your mind? I'd probably assume this is going to be a long and challenging prayer. After all, it's the King of kings, the Master Messiah himself showing us how to pray. This could take a while! But then he starts to pray, and in onds he's done. I'd be thinking, "Was that it? Wow, that was way ⌐ than I was expecting!"

Jesus said we don't have to pray with long, impressive words and vain babbling. He modeled what he taught with this simple, short and thorough expression of prayer.

Relational.

In his book *When We Say Father* Adrian Rogers writes, "Everybody has God all to himself. In fact, God doesn't love us all; He loves us each." He saw prayer as something God initiates in order to commune with us individually and include us in his divine plan. As Dr. Rogers explains it, "The prayer that gets to heaven is the prayer that starts in heaven. We close the circuit. That's all we do...Prayer is the Holy Spirit finding a desire in the heart of the Father, putting that desire into our heart and then sending it back to heaven in the power of the cross."[11] He believed the more time we invest in prayer, the more God's desires will become our desires.

The very first words of the Lord's Prayer are "Our Father." Perhaps the most important purpose of prayer is to *connect* with our Father in heaven. If asking for things were the *only* reason for praying, then the fact that God already knows our needs before we ask could discourage some from praying. It might demotivate us. Could it be that Jesus doesn't want us to make requesting things of him the only goal of our prayers? There is certainly more to prayer than just what we can *get* from it.

Powerful.

Who would think that an acorn the size of a marble could produce a 100-foot-tall oak tree? Or who can imagine the power contained in a paperclip? If turned into pure energy, the atoms in one small paperclip could yield the power of 18,000 tons of TNT explosives![12]

In the same way, who on this earth could fathom the potential power the Lord has made available to us through prayer? And as we will discover in this study, it is not so much the words of our prayers that are powerful; it is the God to whom we pray whose power is beyond all comprehension.

Meditate on the following Scriptures for a few moments.

"Now to him who is able to do far more abundantly than all that we ask or think, according to the power at work within us" (Ephesians 3:20 ESV).

"Call to me and I will answer you, and will tell you great and hidden things that you have not known" (Jeremiah 33:3 ESV).

Now humbly pray the Lord's Prayer aloud. Call on your powerful Father. Be sure your heart connects with him in the quietness of this moment.

Living the Prayer

Again today, plan to pray the Lord's Prayer at least 3 times. Stay in constant communion with him. Seek to pray continually, in every situation. Below, journal a response to what you've learned today.

JOURNAL

During this I could only think about my Mom. When she was sick, I would pray a lot more to ask God to heal her. I always seemed to get the same answer, that he needs her more than I do. So this was the time I learned God's response is not always what we want to hear.

I also think of the time before my car accident. I prayed the model prayer as best I could before I tried crossing the hwy. I had a gut feeling that something bad was coming. I remember telling my mom that I need to go right before that, because someone could get hurt. Then I prayed & that person was me.

DAY 3: *PRAY LIKE THIS*

I've been journaling my quiet times for many years now. One of my favorite things to do is go through books of the Bible and write down what I believe God may be showing me through the Scriptures.

Not long ago I was journaling through the book of Matthew. When I came to chapter 6 and saw the Lord's Prayer, I was tempted to move past it. After all, I've known the Lord's Prayer since I was a kid. I can say it in my sleep I know it so well (or so I thought). As I sat there in my living room that morning, I said to myself, "Since I'm already familiar with this passage, I think I'm just gonna skip it and go on to the next part of chapter 6." I am so glad I didn't do that!

At that moment, a small voice spoke inside my heart and said, "Don't you skip over this part. I have something I want to show you in this today." So, I took a closer look at it. I had to read it over several times, but then I realized something I'd never noticed before. When I finally saw it, it practically jumped off the page at me.

I want you to see if you can notice it too. Please open your Bible and read Matthew 6:7-9. What brief instruction does Jesus give just before he starts the Lord's Prayer? What does he say to set the prayer up for his disciples? (It's short, so don't miss it.)

Each translation is slightly different, but in essence Jesus said in verse 9, "Pray like this." I've read that before. I've heard it preached on. Yet I'd never really thought about it until that moment. As I rolled those words around in my head, my mind began to hearken back to what someone else used to say that was very similar to that. It was my mom.

My mom owned a bakeshop in our backyard for almost as long as I can remember. My dad built the bakery for my mother when I was only 10 years old. She made a good living from that bakery for 36 years. She was well known in our area, and people would drive for hours just to come buy cakes from "Mrs. Virginia." During busy times like the holidays, she would call on me to help her with some baking. I'd tell her, "Mom, you know I'm not good at baking cakes like you are. I can't make them as well as you."

I'll never forget how she would always reply to me. She'd say, "You don't have to do it *exactly* as I do. Just follow my directions and do it *like this*." And then she would show me the recipe and the steps I needed to take to bake the cake. She patiently explained how much of each ingredient to use. And although I never could do it in the exact way she did, I got really close! You could say I learned to bake "like" my mom.

Thinking about that experience with my mother helped me realize something that day during my quiet time. Jesus said to pray "like this." His prayer in Matthew 6 and Luke 11 isn't something I am supposed to mimic in order to do exactly as Jesus did. But I can learn to pray *like* him.

I began to look at the Lord's Prayer more as a recipe or template, if you will, on how to pray. The more I thought about it, the more sense it made to me. There are many wonderful prayers in God's Word that do not use the same words Jesus prayed in the Model Prayer. In John 17 and other passages, Jesus himself prayed words that were different from the Model Prayer. Therefore, it seems clear that Jesus did not intend for us to always pray exactly this, but rather "like" this.

A Pattern Emerges

Sitting there in my living room on the couch that morning, I began to look for natural divisions that might exist in the Model Prayer. If it is really a model for prayer, then what steps can I follow? How can I apply it to my everyday life?

What I'm about to show you has had a profound effect on me. It's affected not only the way I pray but also how I live. It's not too far a stretch to say the Model Prayer has *revolutionized* my prayer life. In fact, what I discovered that unforgettable morning about prayer I have since taught to thousands of church leaders and Christians in several countries. And now it has inspired this Bible study! (Just goes to show we never know what God may have for us if we will set aside consistent time to meet with him and get alone in his Word!)

So let's look closer at a powerful pattern we can glean from the Lord's Prayer. We'll dig deeply into these steps over the next few weeks; but for now, we'll just do a quick overview of each. Here is how each section of what we will call the "prayer model" is labeled:

Vertical

"Our Father which art in heaven, Hallowed be thy name. Thy kingdom come. Thy will be done in earth, as it is in heaven."

Personal

"Give us this day our daily bread. And forgive us our debts, as we forgive our debtors. And lead us not into temptation, but deliver us from evil."

Kingdom

"For thine is the kingdom, and the power, and the glory, for ever. Amen."

To help us remember these divisions more easily, I've named them HE, WE, and THEY:

- HE – Vertical
- WE – Personal
- THEY – Kingdom

We call the first section of the Model Prayer "HE" because it's completely focused on God. Notice there are no references to us at all in this first part.

🎵 Take a marker now and underline every reference to God that you can find in the opening section of the prayer:

"Our Father which art in heaven, Hallowed be thy name. Thy kingdom come. Thy will be done in earth, as it is in heaven."

The second section is called "WE" because the focus suddenly changes from only addressing God to talking about our needs.

🎵 Underline every need Jesus lifted up to God in this second section of the Model Prayer below. Also, circle every instance of the pronouns "us," "we," or "our" that you see.

"Give us this day our daily bread. And forgive us our debts, as we forgive our debtors. And lead us not into temptation, but deliver us from evil."

The last section is called "THEY." This section carries with it the sense that there is something bigger than us and our own concerns.

🎵 What word or words in this final part might cause you to think beyond yourself? Underline any words that could remind you there's something much larger and greater than what we can see.

"For thine is the kingdom, and the power, and the glory, for ever. Amen."

Diving In

Over the next few weeks we are going to dive deep into each of these sections. There are tremendous treasures waiting for us to explore in the beautiful ocean of prayer. The Lord's Prayer is replete with rich theology and practical application.

Today we only skimmed the surface. Nonetheless, I hope you can already see the great potential the Model Prayer has as a guide map for us. It can change not only our prayer lives; we will discover how it can impact our whole lives, leading us to bring greater glory to the Father!

Praying the Prayer

Please journal a prayer in each section below.

HE – Vertical

Praise the Father and surrender to his will. Try not to refer to yourself as you journal this first section of prayer. Keep it vertical, focused on the Lord.

JOURNAL

WE – Personal

Write down something that concerns you right now. It could be a financial problem or an issue at work or at home. Share your needs as a prayer to God.

JOURNAL

THEY – Kingdom

Pray for someone besides you and your family. It might be your neighbor or someone you go to school or work with. Pray for other people's needs instead of your own now.

Living the Prayer

What have you learned in this lesson that you can apply today? What might the Lord be impressing on you that you need to go and do regarding some of the things you just prayed for? Journal your thoughts below.

DAY 4: *WORSHIPING THROUGH PRAYER*

I have a friend named Donald who is a pastor. He lives in Zambia, a beautiful country in south-central Africa slightly larger than the state of Texas. Donald has a heart for God that is also larger than Texas. I have had the opportunity to coach Donald and work with him in our international ministry for several years. One of my favorite things is hearing Donald pray. Trust me when I say, if you're having a bad day, you want Donald to pray with you. I promise you will be encouraged and fired up by the time he says amen! Somehow Donald always manages to turn his prayers to praise.

That is how it should be when we pray. Prayer, after all, is communion with God. And the more we commune with this awesome and loving Father of ours, the more it should warm our hearts to worship him.

♪ I want you to try something. You've been practicing the Lord's Prayer this week, so I want you to quote it aloud now. As you do, think carefully about what you are saying. Savor every word and be sure you speak to God as you quote the prayer. Imagine him bending over you and listening as you pray to him. Stay focused and intentional all the way to the final amen. See if you sense a stirring building in your heart as you go through the prayer.

So, how was it? Did you feel a stirring inside you when you recited the prayer? The way the Lord's Prayer lifts our thoughts and hearts toward the Father, the way it places our burdens before him, and the uncanny way it climaxes with exuberant adoration and a rousing amen—everything about this amazing model of prayer expresses our complete dependence upon God. One cannot pray the Lord's Prayer in earnest without realizing God is God and we are not. And that ultimately sums up what true worship is—acknowledging and submitting to the one, true Lord.

♪ Please read Psalm 57 now. Notice how David's prayer gradually moved from a desperate cry for help to a God-exalting declaration of praise. Highlight each reference that could be considered an expression of worship and an acknowledgment of who God is.

From the Heart

The word *worship* comes from an old English word, "worthscipe" (or worth-ship). Worship in its simplest form is giving *worth* to something—

something we believe is worthy to have all our attention and affection. We attribute worth to God when we love him with our whole heart, mind, soul and strength (Mark 12:30).

Worshiping Jehovah God involves both acts of obedience and an attitude of love for God and others. For example, praying the Lord's Prayer can be an act of worship, but only if we *mean* the words of the prayer. That is because acts of worship must flow from our hearts of worship. *True* worship means loving him and wanting to obey him and do things that please him.

Paul said, "So, whether you eat or drink, or whatever you do, do all to the glory of God" (1 Corinthians 10:31). Worship is much more than singing or going to church. Worship should be our way of life. From things as common as eating and drinking, to sharing our faith with others and showing love to the unlovable—everything we do can qualify as worship when it flows from hearts that love and honor God above all.

Some might wonder: Why all this talk about worship in a study on the Lord's Prayer. That is simple. It is because "Prayer is primarily an act of worship in which the one praying submits to the authority of the One to whom the prayer is offered."[13] As Dr. John MacArthur explains it, the Model Prayer is "primarily an expression of worship…Prayer is the highest form of worship that an individual can participate in."[14]

Could it be that Jesus knew praying this prayer as a habit in our lives could help form in us a heart of worship? Think about it. What better way to live out the challenging instructions Jesus gave us in the Sermon on the Mount than as a sincere believer worshiping God with all her heart?

Consider these examples from Jesus' sermon in Matthew 5-7:

- Jesus said, "Blessed are the meek," and those who hunger for righteousness, and the merciful, and the pure in heart, and the peacemakers. Each of these qualities is a matter of the heart.
- Jesus said, "Rejoice and be glad" when we're persecuted because of him. However, we can't be glad on the outside if we're not glad on the inside. We can't fake joy; either it's in our hearts or it's not.
- Jesus said, "Let your light shine." For us to want to let our light shine before others, we need a genuine burden for them. And where do such burdens of love and concern reside? In our hearts.
- Jesus said our righteousness should exceed "that of the scribes and Pharisees." According to *Strong's Concordance*, the righteousness Jesus referred to is "integrity, virtue, purity of life, uprightness,

and correctness in thinking, feeling, and acting."[15] None of those things is possible if our hearts are not right with God and committed to him.

- Jesus said we are not to kill or commit adultery, and then he pointed out that the mere intention behind these actions constitutes sin in one's heart.
- Jesus said we should lay up treasures in heaven, "for where your treasure is, there your heart will be also."

These examples make it quite clear that the Lord is concerned about the state of our hearts. To reiterate, I believe one of the main reasons Jesus told his disciples to "pray like this" was to help form in them (and in us) a *heart* that loves and follows God.

To help drive home the idea that prayer should flow from a heart of worship, I want us to consider something Jesus said in Matthew 15. In this passage Jesus was rebuking the Pharisees for their hypocrisy regarding their traditions versus God's laws.

Please read the first 11 verses of Matthew 15 now. Especially notice what Jesus said about their hearts and their worship in verses 8 and 9.

Jesus called the Pharisees' worship "a farce" because it did not come from hearts sold out to God. Their worship was not real. In essence he was saying what comes from our lips should flow from our hearts of worship. That should, of course, include prayer. Prayer from a worshiping heart is the kind of prayer God is sure to hear and answer.

In Matthew 15:8-9 Jesus was quoting the prophet Isaiah. Here is something else Isaiah said:

"Behold, the LORD's hand is not shortened, that it cannot save, or his ear dull, that it cannot hear; but your iniquities have made a separation between you and your God, and your sins have hidden his face from you so that he does not hear" (Isaiah 59:1-2).

Did you catch that last line? That is some bold talk, but it's a truth we need to hear and heed. God will not listen if we harbor sin in our hearts. Unconfessed sin causes our hearts to be far from him. We need to confess and forsake our sins, knowing he is faithful and just to forgive us. Because of his awesome mercy, we can "go right into the presence of God with sincere hearts fully trusting him. For our guilty consciences have been sprinkled with Christ's blood to make us clean..." (Hebrews 10:22a NLT).

Common Ground

Can we worship without praying? Technically yes. Can we pray without worshiping? Again, yes…but not for long. One will always lead to the other. If we pray sincerely it should lead us to worship. If we worship sincerely it will most certainly lead us to pray. This is because authentic worship and prayer have something vitally important in common: They both flow from hearts that commune with God. It is a heart of communion and a desire to fellowship with God which drives us to our knees, draws us to the cross, and causes us to want to yield our lives to him every day.

By the time the wise men came to Jesus he was probably a small child, maybe even 2 or 3 years of age. We're not told for sure, but I find it hard to imagine them not addressing him directly at some point while they were there. I believe it is likely they verbally spoke to him. Here is what we know for sure:

"On coming to the house, they saw the child with his mother Mary, and they bowed down and worshiped him. Then they opened their treasures and presented him with gifts of gold, frankincense and myrrh" (Matthew 2:11).

What a privilege those men had. No wonder they rejoiced with exceeding great joy when they saw the star. They knew they were about to commune with God himself! They got to communicate with Jesus one on one. They worshipped him, essentially *praying* to him.

From what we have studied today, I hope you can see how we cannot separate worship and prayer. They always go hand in hand. And the Lord's Prayer, if prayed as a habit and pattern each day, can help form in us a heart that loves and glorifies God—not just with our lips, but also with our lives.

Praying the Prayer

Yesterday we journaled each section of the Model Prayer. I want us to do that again today. Take your time and be sure what you write comes from your heart that longs to worship the Lord.

HE – Vertical
Praise the Father and surrender to his will. It might help to read or listen to, recite, and/or sing a favorite song or hymn that draws you into

worship, encouraging you to humble yourself before our holy, majestic, worthy God and surrender your heart to him.

WE – Personal

Now write down something that concerns you right now. It could be a financial problem or an issue at work or at home. Share your needs as a prayer to God.

THEY – Kingdom

Pray for someone besides you and your family. It might be your neighbor or someone you go to school or work with. Pray for other people's needs instead of your own now.

Living the Prayer

Psalm 119:164 says, "I will praise you seven times a day because all your regulations are just" (NLT). Think about your day ahead. Schedule seven times that you can praise the Lord throughout the day. You may need to set an alarm to remind you. Do whatever you need to do to help you form a habit of daily, continual praise.

DAY 5: *FASTING AND PRAYER*

As an overfed American I admit I may be one of the least likely candidates to write a lesson on fasting. I have friends in Africa who fast often. In fact, I'm coaching a young leader in Kenya right now who is about to begin a 21-day fast! My nature, however, is to run away from such self-sacrificing notions as fasting. Honestly, I'd rather just say to my more spiritual friends, "Hey, good luck with that. Hope it goes well for you!"

Yet, I cannot deny what Jesus taught in Matthew 6. He didn't say *if* you fast; he said *when* you fast.

Read Matthew 6:9-18 now. Notice how seamlessly Jesus flows from the topic of prayer to that of fasting. Why do you think he would include fasting with his teaching on prayer?

The topic of fasting should be included in any study on the Lord's Prayer because it is so directly tied to prayer. Fasting is the very next thing Jesus talks about in the Sermon on the Mount. Thus, it would be almost impossible to have a thorough discussion about the Model Prayer if we ignore the discipline of fasting.

By including the practice of fasting in his teaching on prayer, Jesus elevated the prayer model. It's more than some obligatory moment at a wedding or church service when we chant the Lord's Prayer together. When accompanied by the practice of biblical fasting, prayer becomes a much more solemn and serious undertaking.

In the verses below, please underline or highlight every reference you see to praying and/or fasting.

"In answer to the disciples' question about why they couldn't drive out a demon, Jesus said to them, 'Because your faith is so small…for I solemnly declare to you that if you have faith like a mustard-seed, you shall say to this mountain, 'Remove from this place to that,' and it will remove; and nothing shall be impossible to you. But an evil spirit of this kind is only driven out by prayer and fasting'" (Matthew 17:20-21 WEY).

"And when they had appointed elders for them in every church, with prayer and fasting they committed them to the Lord in whom they had believed" (Acts 14:23 ESV).

"Then I turned my face to the Lord God, seeking him by prayer and pleas for mercy with fasting and sackcloth and ashes" (Daniel 9:23 ESV).

"But I, when they were sick—I wore sackcloth; I afflicted myself with fasting; I prayed with head bowed on my chest" (Psalm 35:13 ESV).

"When I heard this, I sat down and wept. In fact, for days I mourned, fasted, and prayed to the God of heaven…And at the evening sacrifice I rose from my fasting, with my garment and my cloak torn, and fell upon my knees and spread out my hands to the LORD my God" (Ezra 9:3, 5 ESV).

"While they were worshiping the Lord and fasting, the Holy Spirit said, 'Set apart for me Barnabas and Saul for the work to which I have called them.' Then after fasting and praying they laid their hands on them and sent them off" (Acts 13:2-3 ESV).

℘ Why do you think prayer was so often coupled with fasting in the Bible? Was it mostly out of habit and tradition, or could it have been something deeper? How are those two words related?

From God's perspective, fasting is a valuable part of his children's prayer experience. It helps demonstrate to the Lord that we're serious about our requests, serious about our needs, and resolute about connecting with our Father.

Reasons to Fast

We are told in Matthew 4 that Jesus spent forty days and nights in the wilderness fasting and praying before being tempted by the devil. Can you imagine going without any food for forty whole days? Clearly, Jesus put a high priority on fasting. So, if fasting was so vital to Jesus, how much more important should it be for us?

℘ Below are some motivations for fasting. Notice how all of these involve prayer. As you read through this list, highlight the ones that resonate most with you as reasons *you* need to fast.

- Expressing repentance is perhaps the most common reason to fast. King Ahab "sold himself to do what was evil in the sight of the Lord" in 1 Kings 21. But when Elijah confronted him he "humbled himself" with fasting, and God delayed impending disaster.
- Desperation for a request is another reason, to help us seek

God for something we desperately need. David fasted after he committed adultery with Bathsheba and murdered her husband. He repented of his sins and prayed earnestly for his baby not to die.

- A burden for others can prompt us to fast. Prophets in the Old Testament would often fast and pray, putting ashes on their heads for days at a time as they prayed for their nation and their people.
- A desire for communion and closer fellowship with God are also valid reasons to fast. Fasting can be a powerful way to deepen our worship of God. Luke 2 tells the story of an 84-year-old prophetess named Anna. Verse 37 says, "She never left the temple but worshiped night and day, fasting and praying." Anna was devoted to God, and fasting was one expression of her love for him.

Practical Tips

As you can probably see, one would be hard pressed to be a true worshiper who seeks a stronger relationship with the Lord and a better understanding of God if we never practice fasting. No wonder Jesus said, "*When* you fast..." (italics added).

Therefore, to help prepare for *when* you fast, here are a few tips...

- Think ahead a bit. While you shouldn't share publicly about your fasting, those directly affected may need a heads-up. For example, if your spouse or family member prepares meals for you, it might be considerate to tell him or her your plans so they won't prepare food unnecessarily. It can also be a good idea to inform a friend who can hold you accountable to your commitment.
- It's important to understand the limits of your body. Health experts tell us we can go about 3 weeks without food and maybe 3-4 days without water. There is a limit to what our bodies can endure. And if we are in poor health, we should consider limiting our fasting time even more.
- Although fasting in the Bible usually meant denying oneself food, fasts don't have to involve only food or water. I think the broader application is that we deprive ourselves of something we enjoy. I've had friends who've fasted from Facebook and social media for several days, or from playing video games, or from drinking sweet tea. The key is abstaining from something for a period of

time so we can use that time instead to focus our energies on the Lord and on prayer.

- Fasting should not only mean saying no to certain things. It should also include saying *yes* to some things. This is vitally important. For example, while you are fasting, be sure to intensify the amount you pray. When you might normally be eating, invest that time alone with God instead. Silence your cell phone and other things that might distract you. Focus on the Lord. Earnestly seek him with your whole heart.

Living the Prayer

In his book, *A Hunger for God*, John Piper writes, "If we don't feel strong desires for the manifestation of the glory of God, it is not because we have drunk deeply and are satisfied. It is because we have nibbled so long at the table of the world. Our soul is stuffed with small things, and there is no room for the great." He goes on to say, "There is an appetite for God. And it can be awakened."[16]

Decide today to delve deeper into your worship of the Lord. Decide to awaken your appetite to know and love God more through fasting.

Praying the Prayer

Let's close by praying through each section of the Model Prayer. Please take your time. Use this as an opportunity to connect with the Lord and commune with him.

HE – Vertical

Enjoy a sweet time of worship with the Father. Surrender yourself to his will. Listen to him as he speaks to your heart, perhaps about fasting. Maybe the words of this worship song express your surrender today:

Lord, you are more precious than silver
Lord, you are more costly than gold
Lord, you are more beautiful than diamonds
And nothing I desire compares with you.[17]

WE – Personal

Now write about something that currently concerns you, possibly a lost family member or a personal problem. Share your needs as a prayer to God and consider this: How might fasting give strength to your prayers?

JOURNAL

THEY – Kingdom

Pray for those outside your circle of friends and family, maybe a Facebook acquaintance who has posted a prayer request or your child's teacher who has been ill. Perhaps there is a global issue that you feel the need to pray about. Ask your heavenly Father, whom you've just communed with, what you should focus on during this part of your prayer time. Journal your prayer.

JOURNAL

WEEK 1 FOLLOW-UP QUESTIONS FOR GROUP DISCUSSION

1. What do you think the Lord's Prayer has to do with worship?
2. What does the Model Prayer mean to you personally? Have there been times in your life when hearing it or reading it touched you deeply?
3. What is something you need to work on in your own prayer life?
4. How do you hope to benefit from this study?
5. Share a time when you knew for sure prayer was "real."
6. Is it easy or difficult to listen during your prayer time? Why do you think that's true for you?
7. Describe your ideal prayer setting: time, place, environment, accoutrements (music, cup of coffee, journal, crackling fire). How does that differ from your actual prayer setting?
8. How powerful would you say your prayers are? Why?
9. Which section of the Model Prayer—HE, WE, or THEY—are you most comfortable or familiar with? Why do you think that is?
10. Which section of the Model Prayer are you least familiar with, or which section do you expect to struggle with most? Why do you think that is?
11. Do you agree with this quote? "Worship is much more than singing or going to church. Worship should be our way of life."
12. On pages 18-19, which of the passages about worship being a matter of the heart resonates most with you? Why?
13. What do you think is achieved by fasting? Why do you think fasting helps achieve that outcome?

Footnotes for Week 1:

[1] Andrew Murray, *With Christ in the School of Prayer* (Ohio: Barbour and Company, 1992), 24.

[2] Tertullian, *Fathers of the Church*, vol. 40, 159; vol. 36, 133.

[3] Quoted in *Martin Luther: Selections from His Writings* (ed. John Dillenberger; New York: Doubleday, 1962), p. 226; from Work, Ain't Too Proud to Beg, p. xiv.

[4] Albert Mohler, "Prayer, Piety, and the Glory of God: The Lord's Prayer in the 21st Century," *AlbertMohler.com*, June 19, 2018, https://albertmohler.com/2018/06/19/prayer-piety-glory-god-lords-prayer-21st-century.

[5] Matthew Henry, "Matthew Henry Commentary on Matthew 6:5-8," *Bible Hub*, https://biblehub.com/commentaries/matthew/6-5.htm.

[6] "Atheist Prayer: Religious Activity Not Uncommon Among Unbelievers," *Huffington Post*, June 26, 2013, https://www.huffingtonpost.com/2013/06/25/athiest-prayer_n_3498365.html.

[7] Albert Mohler, "Prayer, Piety, and the Glory of God: The Lord's Prayer in the 21st Century," *AlbertMohler.com*, June 19, 2018, https://albertmohler.com/2018/06/19/prayer-piety-glory-god-lords-prayer 21st century.

[8] "Forms Of Prayer In The Religions Of The World," *Britannica*, https://www.britannica.com/topic/prayer/Forms-of-prayer-in-the-religions-of-the-world.

[9] Max Lucado, *Before Amen: The Power of a Simple Prayer* (Nashville: Thomas Nelson Publishers, 2014), chapter 1 (e-book).

[10] E.M. Bounds, *E.M. Bounds on Prayer* (Massachusetts: Hendrickson Publishers, 2006), Chapter 2 (e-book).

[11] Adrian Rogers, *When We Say Father: Unlocking the Power of the Lord's Prayer* (Nashville: B&H Publishing Group, 2108), chapter 7 (e-book).

[12] "The Power of Tiny Things Answer Key," *Nova Science Programming on Air and Online*, https://www.pbs.org/wgbh/nova/einstein/tiny-answers.html.

[13] Dwight Pentecost, *Thy Kingdom Come: Tracing God's Kingdom Program and Covenant Promises Throughout History* (Grand Rapids: Kregel, 1995), 242.

[14] John Macarthur, "Prayer: The Highest Form of Worship," *Grace to You*, August 26, 2012, https://www.gty.org/library/sermons-library/90-447/prayer-the-highest-form-of-worship.

[15] Strong's Concordance, 1343 Dikaiosuné, *Bible Hub*, https://biblehub.com/greek/1343.htm.

[16] John Piper, *A Hunger for God: Desiring God through Fasting and Prayer* (Wheaton, Illinois: Crossway, 1997) 25, 26.

[17] Lynne DeShazo, *More Precious Than Silver* (Integrity's Hosannah! Music, 1982).

WEEK 2 VERTICAL PRAYER

*Our Father which art in heaven, Hallowed be thy name. Thy kingdom
come. Thy will be done in earth, as it is in heaven.*
Matthew 6:9b-10 KJV

DAY 1 *OUR FATHER*

Have you ever tried to describe to someone a beautiful vacation spot
where you've never been yourself? It's kind of hard to explain a place you
have never seen or experienced, isn't it? In the same way, it is not enough
to talk about prayer or dream about prayer. Like S.M. Lockridge said in his
famous sermon *That's My King*, "You have to pray in order to pray!"[1]

In a sermon on the Lord's Prayer, C.H. Spurgeon said, "It seems to me
that Christ gave it as a model, whereby we are to fashion all our prayers…
It is a map; but a man is not a traveler because he puts his fingers across
the map. And so a man may use this form of prayer, and yet be a total
stranger to the great design of Christ in teaching it to his disciples."[2]

Our purpose in going through this study is to avoid being strangers to
God's great design for prayer.

In last week's lessons we overviewed the Model Prayer or the "map,"
as Spurgeon called it. We learned about the three divisions or steps of the
prayer model: HE, WE and THEY. We ran our fingers across the map, so
to speak, and we now know the course we must take. This week, we will
set out on that great adventure! And the first leg of our exciting journey is
a "heavenly highway" that can lead us straight to the *Father*.

Before we start today's lesson, let's first stop and pray and ask the
Lord to show us how we might improve our prayer life. Pray now and ask
the Father to open your eyes to the amazing truths he wants to show you

in his Word this week.

The Model Prayer begins "Our Father, who is in heaven." Everything else about this prayer is dependent on us grasping these first, all-important words. They are key to getting us on the road to a life of powerful prayer and fellowship with God.

To help us better appreciate the impact of Jesus' opening words, we need to look back to some of the prayers from great prophets and saints in the Old Testament.

- Hezekiah began his prayer with "O LORD, God of Israel..." (2 Kings 19:15).
- Solomon also prayed "Lord, the God of Israel..." (2 Chronicles 6:14).
- King Asa started with a simple "LORD..." (2 Chronicles 14:11).
- Jehoshaphat stood up in the assembly of Judah and said, "O LORD, God of our fathers..." (2 Chronicles 20:6).
- Daniel prayed, "O Lord, the great and awesome God..." (Daniel 9:4).
- Nehemiah prayed similarly "O LORD, God of heaven..." (Nehemiah 1:5).
- Ezra's prayer was more personal. He began his prayer with "O my God..." (Ezra 9:5).
- Like King Asa, Habakkuk simply started with "LORD..." (Habakkuk 3:2).
- At the beginning of Psalm 25 David prayed, "To you, O LORD...O my God..."

What do all of these verses have in common? They are all prayers directed to God. Yet none of them addressed him as Father. In fact, there's not one prayer in the Old Testament that refers to God in that way. Isn't that interesting?

Paradigm Shifts

Did you know the first recorded prayer which calls on God as "Our Father" does not happen until the New Testament? In the Sermon on the Mount, Jesus, in his Model Prayer, addressed God as Father for the first time in Scripture.

Talk about a shift of paradigm! Jesus came on the scene and, boom, he did something few had done before: He addressed God directly with a word which, up to that time, had rarely been uttered when calling upon

God. "Father" is used for God only 15 times in the entire Old Testament! Most people today are accustomed to hearing God referred to as Father. Many of us grew up quoting the Lord's Prayer and hearing him addressed as Father; so perhaps we don't find it to be so shocking. But imagine how the disciples must have felt. They weren't as familiar with that title for God as we are.

Yet now, as Jesus taught his disciples to pray, he spoke directly to God and called him "Father." What's more, he instructed his disciples to do the same. It may have been quite startling for them to hear Jesus begin his prayer in such a unique and intimate way.

But addressing God as Father in the Model Prayer reflected more than just a shift in the degree of intimacy between God and his creation. Additionally, using the word Father for God signaled a huge divergence from what had traditionally been emphasized by the religious rulers of the day. Think about the prayers we read a few moments ago from the Old Testament. The emphasis in those prayers was on God's greatness. Religion in the Old Testament and during the time between the Testaments was more about God's holiness and "the fear of the Lord."

Jesus, however, brought a new perspective. When he came, he moved the focus away from religion and toward a *relationship*. By telling the disciples to address God as "our Father," Jesus invited his followers to share in the same relationship with God he had. In Galatians 4, Paul writes, "... God sent his Son...to buy freedom for us who were slaves to the law, so that he could adopt us as his very own children" (v. 4-5). Imagine that! We can be adopted into God's great big, awesome family. We can call him "our Father." What a privilege!

Great Benefits

Why is it so important to acknowledge God as Father? Let's consider some blessings that go along with this amazing, vertical relationship.

First, if God is our Father we have *authority* to approach him in prayer.

Please read John 1:9-13. Notice verse 12. What has been given to those who have believed on Christ and accepted him? According to verse 13, how do we become children of God?

God wants to grant us the right to be called his children. Unlike many seem to believe, being his child is not automatic. We are not all God's children. Only those who are born of God can be called his children, only

32

those who put their trust in Jesus as Savior and Lord. In John 14:6 Jesus made this clear: "I am the way, the truth, and the life. No one can come to the Father except through me."

Those who are God's adopted children can enjoy a second incredible benefit: *accessibility* to his throne of grace. In the Old Testament, only the Levite priests could go into the Holy of Holies. But now, adoption as his sons and daughters grants us complete access to God, any time of any day! Listen to what Hebrews 10 says about that: "We can boldly enter heaven's Most Holy Place because of the blood of Jesus. By his death, Jesus opened a new and life-giving way through the curtain into the Most Holy Place. And since we have a great High Priest who rules over God's house, let us go right into the presence of God with sincere hearts fully trusting him" (v. 19-22a).

In one of our recent mission trips, we had the privilege to meet a distinguished member of the Zambian Parliament, the Honorable Dr. Martin Malama. We met Dr. Malama at a radio station in Zambia where we were doing an interview about NLW's leadership training in Africa. He invited our team to eat with him at the Parliament headquarters. We could hardly believe we had been given such an opportunity!

When we arrived, we were ushered right in to where several dignitaries were enjoying lunch. After the meal, Dr. Malama asked us to go with him to the Parliament prayer meeting being held in an adjacent building. We walked through several guard checks, but no one searched us or asked us questions. After the prayer meeting, Dr. Malama invited us to go with him into the chambers where Parliament was meeting with the President of Zambia. Again, no one stopped us or questioned us in any way. We simply showed them our passports, logged our names in their record book, and proceeded right into Parliament. It was that easy.

Why did they allow us into their high-level meetings? It certainly wasn't because of any credentials we had (we had none!). It was only because we were with Dr. Malama. To anyone who asked him about us, he would simply say, "They're with me." We had total access because of our relationship with this high-ranking government official.

And so it is with us, as God's children. We are with Jesus! Jesus is our Brother. And through the blood he shed for us we have access to the very presence of the Father.

Prodigal Prayers

It is important to note that this access is not dependent on our own righteousness and good works. I think some Christians feel they have to clean up their act before they can pray to God. But that is not what the Bible teaches.

༄ Look at Hebrews 4:14-16 now. Pay special attention to verse 16. How and why are we to come to God's throne?

We don't need to confess our sins first, and then come before God. According to Hebrews 4:16, we come boldly to him in order *to receive mercy*. It is when we bow before him in his throne room of grace that he shows us our sins and faults. It is there that he grants us mercy and forgiveness.

At some point in our lives, we can all probably relate to feeling a little like the prodigal Jesus talked about in Luke 15. Listen in verse 20 to how the father responded when his renegade son finally decided to come back home: "While he was still a long way off, his father saw him coming. Filled with love and compassion, he ran to his son, embraced him, and kissed him."

Access to God is based entirely on our relationship with him as our Father. It doesn't matter what we've done or not done. It doesn't matter how foolish we may have acted or how offensive toward God our thoughts have been. We are still his children, and our Father still loves us just the same. Do you see now why it is so vital that we understand and embrace God in this way as we start our prayers to him? Knowing and acknowledging God as Father is truly the gateway to everything else we will pray in the Model Prayer and in our lives.

Praying the Prayer

We don't have to be perfect when we come to God, and neither do our prayers. I love what Spurgeon said: "Our prayers are little broken things; we cannot put them together, but our Father, he will hear us. Oh! what a beginning is 'Our Father'...since he is my Father, he will, he must hear my prayers."[3]

What is it about God as Father that makes you glad? Take a few minutes to journal a prayer to God thanking him for being Father and Lord. Pour out your broken, less-than-perfect prayers to him as you pray through the steps in the Model Prayer today.

HE – Vertical

Remember to try not to refer to your needs and personal concerns as you journal this first stage of prayer, which is your time to honor and adore the King and surrender yourself to him. Keep it vertical, focused on the Lord.

WE – Personal

Write down something that concerns you right now. It could be a financial problem or an issue at work or at home. Share your needs as a prayer to God.

THEY – Kingdom

Pray for someone besides you and your family. It might be your neighbor or someone you go to school or work with. Pray for other people's needs instead of your own now.

Are you certain God is your Father? Do you know for sure that you have a relationship with his Son, Jesus, as your Savior?

If not, pray to him now. 1. Admit you are a sinner. 2. Believe in your heart that Jesus died for you and that he rose again and is alive today. 3. Confess your need of him in your life. Ask him to forgive your sin and come into your life and save you.

If you prayed that prayer for the first time, he just saved you! "For all who call upon the name of the Lord shall be saved" (Romans 10:13). Be sure to call or message someone today and let them know of your decision.

JOURNAL

DAY 2: ABBA

J.I. Packer writes, "If you want to judge how well a person understands Christianity, find out how much he makes of the thought of being God's child, and having God as his Father."[4] We learned yesterday that understanding and embracing God as our Father is vitally important as we pray through the Model Prayer. It's so important, in fact, that I think we need to invest another day on it.

Please join me in praying now that the Holy Spirit would help move this amazing truth of God as our Father from our heads down into our hearts: "Holy Lord, I thank you for revealing yourself to me, for sending your only Son to take my place on the cross and show me your amazing heart of love for this world. Please teach *me* to know and embrace you as the one and only loving, just, kind, good and holy Father that you are. Please help this relationship become a deep and lasting reality in my heart and soul. In the name of Jesus, we pray. Amen."

One of my favorite movies is *The Patriot,* an epic historical fiction film directed by Roland Emmerich and starring Mel Gibson. The story centers around Gibson's character, Benjamin Martin, a colonist-turned-hero in the American Revolutionary War, who was reluctantly swept into the war by the murder of one of his sons.

I've watched this movie several times over the years. There is one scene about mid-way through the movie that always grips me. It involves Benjamin's youngest daughter, Susan. She's around 5 years old. He hasn't heard her speak a word in the 3 years since her mother's death. In this powerful scene, Benjamin is leaving his children yet again to go to the front lines of battle. Here's how this emotional moment plays out:

> Benjamin's family stands in a line as he says goodbye to each of them. Then he sees Susan standing a few feet away. He motions to her, but she doesn't move. He walks over to her, kneels down and gently hugs her, saying, "Just a little goodbye? One word? That's all I want to hear." But Susan remains silent, standing with her arms at her sides, not responding to his embrace. Finally, Benjamin lets go of her. She just stares at him. He mounts up and starts to ride away, but as he's about to round a curve and disappear, Susan suddenly cries out, "Papa!" With halting steps at first, then faster and faster, she runs down the path toward her

father. "Papa, don't go! I'll say anything." Benjamin stops and turns when he hears Susan running after him. With her eyes filled with tears, Susan says, "Please, Papa, I'll say anything you want!" Benjamin spurs his horse straight toward her. Then he dismounts and runs to meet her. Susan pleads again, "Please, Papa, please don't go…. I'll talk to you, I'll say anything you want, just tell me what you want me to say, I'll say anything, I promise, please, Papa, just stay…" The words tumble from her as fast as she can get them out. Her father then wraps his sobbing child in his arms, holding her, covering her with kisses, and letting her cry—all the while fighting back tears of his own.

I'm not really one to cry much, but I tear up almost every time I watch this scene. It's like something moves me deep inside when I watch it. I think what makes this scene so powerful for me is the word "papa." Every time Susan says it, it rips my heart out. It makes this whole moment seem more real and relatable.

⚯ Try going back now and rereading that scene. This time, though, replace "papa" with the word "father."

Just doesn't quite have the same impact, does it? "Father" seems more formal and removed. On the other hand, "papa" shows affection, endearment, and intimacy. Susan repeatedly calling her dad "papa" reveals her deep affection and longing for her father. So it's only natural for viewers (like me) to be drawn in and affected by such love. It's enough to make a grown man cry!

Intimate Name

Whenever I hear the word "papa" I am reminded of an amazing word in the New Testament: Abba, a word many theologians translate as "papa." According to Strong's Concordance, Abba is "the term of tender endearment by a beloved child…in an affectionate, dependent relationship with their father."[5]

We already know that "Father" was Jesus' favorite name for God. In fact, he began the Model Prayer addressing God as Father. There he used a Greek word for "father" that refers to one who is in "intimate connection and relationship."[6] When Jesus prayed to his Father in the Garden of Gethsemane he included the Aramaic word *Abba*, which helps us sense Jesus' deep relationship with God. Listen to what Mark writes: "He went on a little farther and fell to the ground. He prayed that, if it were possible, the awful hour awaiting him might pass him by. 'Abba, Father,' he cried out, 'everything is possible for you. Please take this cup of suffering away from me. Yet I want your will to be done, not mine'" (Mark 14:35 NLT).

Calling God by this unique name is striking. There is no evidence in pre-Christian Jewish literature that Jews addressed God as "Abba." Jesus introduced a new way of praying and talking to God that is as natural, intimate and sincere as a child talking with his or her father.[7]

℘ Like Jesus, Paul also refers to God as Abba, Father—twice to be exact, in Romans and also in Galatians. We need to read both passages carefully to help us absorb their powerful truths. Let's start with Romans 8:14-16. Notice how much Paul mentions the Spirit in this passage.

℘ Now go to Galatians and read 4:4-6. Compare verse 6 to Romans 8:15. At first glance it might appear that Paul repeats himself regarding his teaching on Abba, Father. But look closer. Do you see the change in the subject? Who does Paul say is doing the crying in each of these verses?

In Romans Paul says, "...we cry, 'Abba! Father!'" But in Galatians he indicates that the *Spirit* is the One who cries through us. So, which is it? Is it us or the Spirit who cries? Is Paul contradicting himself? Not at all, for those two ideas work hand in hand. It is both us and the Spirit *through* us that cry "Abba."

Affirming Spirit

The reality is that we can do nothing apart from the Spirit helping us—not even pray. In the verse right before Romans 8:15 Paul says, "We are led by the Spirit of God." Then further down in Romans 8, Paul emphasizes the importance of the Spirit in our prayers when he writes, "... we don't know what God wants us to pray for. But the Holy Spirit prays for us with groanings that cannot be expressed in words" (v. 26 NLT). As one theologian puts it, "Acceptable prayer is wrought in us by the Spirit."[8] We simply cannot enjoy a deep, intimate fellowship with Almighty God without the Holy Spirit.

The Spirit wants to pray through us, but only if we allow him to. Prayer is still our choice. We can hinder prayer from going up to God, just as we can stop our praise to him. David must have understood this, because in Psalm 51 he prayed, "O Lord, open my lips, and my mouth will declare your praise" (v. 15). He knew his sin was keeping his praise from flowing freely to God. David chose to confess his sin and ask God to unseal his lips. So it is with our prayers. We can stop the flow of prayer in our lives if we are hiding sin in our hearts. We can feel so guilty or be so distracted that we do not even take time to pray and acknowledge our heavenly Father. It is a sad reality for many.

There's one more verse in Romans 8 that I want to highlight. Verse 16 says, "For his Spirit joins with our spirit to affirm that we are God's children." Remember what I said about the scene in *The Patriot*, how I feel like something moves me deep inside when I watch it? Turns out something does! It's actually *someone*. Paul sums up perfectly what happens inside of me: It is God's Spirit affirming my spirit.

I wish I could adequately describe the joy and peace which comes from knowing I am a child of God. But honestly, words escape me. Apparently, Spurgeon struggled to express how he felt too. "What is the spirit of adoption, whereby we cry 'Abba, Father'?" Spurgeon reflected. "I cannot tell you; but if you have felt it you will know it...It is a sacred touch of nature, a throb in the breast that God has put there, and that cannot be taken away. It is a sweet compound of faith that knows God to be my Father, of love that loves him as my Father, joy that rejoices in him as my Father, fear that trembles to disobey him because he is my Father, and a confident affection and trustfulness that relies upon him."[9]

No wonder John exclaims, "See how very much our Father loves us, for he calls us his children, and that is what we are!" (1 John 3:1 NLT).

Praying the Prayer

I want us to journal each section of the Model Prayer again today. Please take your time and be sure what you write comes from a heart that longs to worship the Lord.

HE – Vertical
There is a worship song with these words:
> You're a good, good father; that's who you are...And I'm loved by you; that's who I am...It's love so undeniable, I, I can hardly speak. Peace so unexplainable, I, I can hardly think, as you call me deeper still...into love, love, love.[10]

Today, as you praise God, approach him as you would a good, good father who has a deep, abiding love for you and desires the intimate relationship of a parent with you. If you have trouble relating to God in this way, for whatever reason, today would be a good day to work on your relationship with your Abba Father—your Papa!

JOURNAL

WE – Personal

Seek your Abba's help with meeting your needs and the needs of those you love. Perhaps you can think of someone close to you who desperately needs to know God as his or her Abba Father and could focus on that person today.

JOURNAL

THEY – Kingdom

This is your time to pray for people and about situations outside your immediate realm of concern. Who would benefit by having a relationship with our Abba Father? What situation in your world, nation, state, or church would benefit from the intervention of our Almighty God?

Living the Prayer

Intimacy with our Father is both awesome and attainable, but it is something we need to work to cultivate. Dr. Charles Swindoll suggests four disciplines to help us develop deeper intimacy with God.[11] I've listed them below. Beside each one, write something you can do *this week* to help you focus more on God.

- *Simplicity, which requires reordering our lives.* How can you simplify your to-do list this week to have more time for the Lord and his Word?

- *Silence, which asks us to be still.* When this week can you be silent and still for at least an hour?

- *Solitude, which involves being alone with God.* When this week can you set aside extra time to read God's Word and pray?

- *Surrender, which beckons us to let go.* What in your life might be holding you back from experiencing deep fellowship with the Lord? What might you need to confess and forsake?

DAY 3: *IN HEAVEN*

"Don't make rash promises, and don't be hasty in bringing matters before God. After all, God is in heaven, and you are here on earth. So let your words be few" (Ecclesiastes 5:2 NLT).

♫ Please read that verse again. And again. And maybe one more time. Let those solemn words soak down into your soul as we begin this lesson.

♫ Now, slowly read the lyrics to the song below. Consider letting this be your prayer today...

> You are God in heaven
> And here am I on earth
> So I'll let my words be few
> Jesus, I am so in love with You
> And I'll stand in awe of You, Jesus
> Yes, I'll stand in awe of You
> And I'll let my words be few
> Jesus, I am so in love with You [12]

We've learned this week that the "fear of the Lord" was a dominating theme in the Old Testament. People were to keep their distance when in the presence of a holy God. However, in the New Testament because of Jesus' sacrifice, we can have boldness and confidence as believers to come near to God as Father.[13] Jesus emphasized the Fatherhood of God. As we have noted, "Father" was his favorite term for addressing God.[14]

Jesus didn't come to abolish the law of the Old Testament. He came to *fulfill* it. His emphasis on intimacy with the Father didn't negate our need to revere God as both holy and worthy of veneration. When Jesus spoke of "Our Father who is in heaven," he seemed to be indicating we should have a deep reverence for the Father.

I have a good friend named Herb who is an adjunct professor at a seminary in New Orleans. You don't have to talk long with Herb before you'll hear him bring up one of his favorite topics: worshiping God as high and exalted. As he puts it, everyone should "focus first on God's glory and other transcendent characteristics [which means they are not subject to the limitations of the material universe]. This contextualizes our corporate worship and our lives individually when we realize he is the King."[15] I love Herb's passion for God's glory because I know that what he says is true. Unfortunately, such reverence as Herb speaks of is often overlooked in our modern worship planning and leading.

As in our worship, we also should not miss the importance of acknowledging the Lord's transcendent nature in our prayers. In fact, if we only say "Our Father" and we skip the qualifying clause "who is in heaven," then our prayers can quickly become derailed and lose their power and effectiveness.

Both Here and High

That is not to imply we always have to say "who is in heaven" when we pray or that God is literally only in heaven. Quite the contrary. He is there in the room with you now, and he is here with me as I write these words. What it means is that he is high above our thoughts and ways. That is the mindset and the heart-set we must begin with as we focus on our Father. One commentator summed it up like this: Praying "our Father," we express his nearness to us; praying "who is in heaven," we acknowledge his distance from us. Holy, loving familiarity is suggested in the first one; awe-filled reverence in the other.[16]

Listen to what Paul writes in Ephesians: "Because of Christ and our faith in him, we can now come boldly and confidently into God's presence. So please don't lose heart because of my trials here. I am suffering for you, so you should feel honored. When I think of all this, I fall to my knees and pray to the Father, the Creator of everything in heaven and on earth" (3:12-15 NLT). Notice how Paul talks of boldly entering God's presence, while also bowing in humility before his Father when he prays.

Turn to Isaiah 6 now and read verses 1-8. What do you suppose prompted Isaiah to volunteer when he heard God ask who would go for him? What did Isaiah experience in his vision that may have changed his perspective?

Isaiah was a prophet who knew God and spoke for God. Yet he still needed to be reminded that God is on a lofty throne. In the midst of that season of discouragement and grief with the passing of his friend, King Uzziah, he needed to lift his mind toward heaven. Before he had any communion with God in this scene, before there was any conversation or expressed desire to serve God, Isaiah first envisioned the Lord on his throne.

That should be our progression as we approach God. We should seek to know him first as our Father who is exalted above all else. Like Isaiah, we too need to acknowledge God as high and lifted up. This is a vital part of the first step—the HE part—of the prayer model.

Can You Imagine?

Read Revelation 1:9-18 now. If you were John in this scene, would Jesus' words to John bring you comfort and cause you not to fear?

Have you ever been outside late at night with a friend, and you heard something in the woods that frightened you? Your friend says with a shaky voice, "Don't be afraid. We'll be okay. I'm here." You appreciate your friend trying to comfort you. But the fact is, your friend is no bigger or stronger than you. She couldn't really help you. Having your friend there doesn't really keep you from being afraid because she is as scared as you are!

Put yourself in John's place. You see Jesus, his eyes like flames of fire and his face shining like the brilliant sun. Almost involuntarily you fall lifeless at his feet. This person is nothing like your friend in the woods. No, this is God Almighty. Then he lays his right hand on you and says, "Don't be afraid! I am the First and the Last. I am the living one. I died, but look—I am alive forever and ever! And I hold the keys of death and the grave."

How would that make you feel? This isn't some wimpy, anemic god trying to comfort you. This is the true and living Christ in all his glory. When God himself says we don't need to be afraid, we don't need to be afraid. Notice that Jesus didn't lose any of his glory, eminence and transcendence in that moment, even though he spoke with John one on one. This was a very personal encounter with the Living God. Jesus even reached out and lovingly touched him.

Do you see now why it's so vital that we lift our spiritual eyes above some humanistic view of who we think God is? He's not limited like human fathers here on earth. He is our Father in heaven.

In Awe

What differences might it make in your prayer life if the phrase "Who is in heaven" didn't exist? What if Jesus had never included those words in the Model Prayer? Imagine that you didn't realize the Father you prayed to is the great, all-powerful God. Would you still bring him your burdens and your fears? Would you seek his direction? What impact might that have on how you pray and what you pray for? Take time to write out your thoughts.

God meets with us in prayer; yet he doesn't dethrone himself in order to commune with us. In fact, he never leaves his throne. He always has been and still is the King of kings and Lord of lords. Moreover, he is also our Father who loves us completely, unconditionally, undeniably, unfathomably, and eternally. What a comfort that should be to anyone who is his child!

In *Praying the Lord's Prayer*, J.I. Packer writes, "The vitality of prayer lies largely in the vision of God that prompts it...Knowing that our Father God is in heaven...[increases] our wonder, joy, and a sense of privilege at being his children and being given a hotline of prayer for communication with him."[17] I love what Max Lucado says: "When Christ is great, our fears are not. As awe of Jesus expands, fears of life diminish."[18]

In Week 3 of our study we'll turn our focus to the second part of the Model Prayer. That's where we get to commit to him our own needs and burdens. I really need that part of the prayer, don't you? But before we can take that next step in the Model Prayer though, it is essential we first have a healthy dose of awe for God. It is not enough to pray to him as our Father. We need to qualify what kind of Father he is. We need to embrace and trust him as the one and only true God who is forever high and lifted up.

Lord, please increase our awe of you—our Father who is *in heaven*!

Praying the Prayer

Take a few minutes to journal each section of the Model Prayer again today. It's vital that we build a strong habit of praying like this.

HE – Vertical
Surrender your will to our Father in heaven and praise him aloud today! You might want to accept the Psalmist's exuberant invitation to worship:

> "Praise the LORD. Praise God in his sanctuary; praise him
> in his mighty heavens. Praise him for his acts of power; praise
> him for his surpassing greatness. Praise him with the sounding
> of the trumpet, praise him with the harp and lyre, praise him
> with timbrel and dancing, praise him with the strings and pipe,

praise him with the clash of cymbals, praise him with resounding cymbals. Let everything that has breath praise the LORD" (Psalm 150:1-6 NIV).

Now journal your own words of praise.

JOURNAL

WE – Personal

What's something that is burdening you right now? Do you believe that the God described in the Scripture above can handle that need? Journal about the problem and your prayer asking for God's help.

JOURNAL

THEY – Kingdom

Think of others you know who might have a burden as great as yours or greater. Go in prayer to our mighty Father in heaven and ask him to intervene.

Living the Prayer

In C.S. Lewis' book, *Prince Caspian*, Lucy sees Aslan, the lion, for the first time in many years. He has changed since their last encounter, and his size surprises her.

"Aslan," said Lucy, "you're bigger."

"That is because you are older, little one." answered he.

"Not because you are?"

"I am not. But every year you grow, you will find me bigger."[19]

Only the Holy Spirit can help you grow and see your Father as bigger and bigger. Only he can illuminate your heart and mind to embrace an almost dualistic concept of God—who is both here with you and also exalted above you. Pray and ask the Spirit to guide you and deepen your understanding of your precious, *heavenly* Father.

DAY 4: *HALLOWED*

Today in the Model Prayer our focus is on the words "Hallowed be your name." *Hallowed* is not a word most of us use. Thus, it may need some explanation. Dr. Vernon Whaley, a member of our Board of Directors at NLW International and a leading authority on biblical worship, explains it like this: "When we make something 'hallowed,' we are acknowledging it as worthy of love, devotion, admiration, or worship…We always hallow (hold in high regard and reverence) His holy name."[20]

The words "Hallowed be your name" have huge significance within the Lord's Prayer. To help us grasp this directive better and understand how we can apply it in our lives, we need to consider three things: why it matters within the Model Prayer, what it means, and where it is placed. Or to put it a different way, we need to study its priority, purpose and position.

Why It Matters

The very fact that praise is securely included within the Lord's Prayer is significant. By including "Hallowed be your name" Jesus set a high precedence on worship as a part of prayer. Praise has always been a huge priority with God. Psalm 22:3 says, "Yet you are holy, enthroned on the praises of Israel." Praise is where God lives. He is at home in praise. He is "great and greatly to be praised" (Psalm 48:1). Think about it: When Jesus prayed, "Hallowed be your name," he was giving intentional, deliberate, and vocal praise to God's greatness and glory. Should we do any less?

Read Psalm 100 now. What can we learn about praise from this chapter, especially verse 4?

One of the first books to influence me and help me understand the priority of praise was *The Hallelujah Factor* by Jack Taylor. He says that "praise, with thanksgiving, is the only access into the presence of God… Worship experience which is begun by or prefaced with praise will consummate in glad fellowship with Holy God…"[4] Isn't that our hope? Shouldn't that be our ultimate goal, to have awesome fellowship with our holy Father? If so, we must make a *habit* of praising him when we pray.

What It Means

Also significant are the specific words Jesus used here. "Hallowed be your name" has been translated as "Your name be honored as holy" (CSB), "May your name be kept holy" (NLT), "Help us to honor your name" (CEV), and "Reveal who you are" (MSG). There are two words in particular that we need to look at closely within this powerful request.

First, notice Jesus' focus on the Father's *name*. In our day and time we don't think much about the meaning of someone's name. A Bible commentator puts it like this: "We tend to look on a name almost as an accidental appendage by which a person is designated."[21] (I can relate to that. My name seems pretty accidental to me. It has no real meaning, and my parents clearly put little thought into it. Fact is, I was named after a guy my older sister had a crush on at the time! No kidding.)

In Bible times, however, names were a big deal. A person's name represented his nature and qualities. That is especially true of God's names. The "name" of God summarized all his revealed names. His name stands for God and for all that he is. When Jesus invoked God's name in the Model Prayer, he was using it to represent God's character and attributes.

The other word to point out in this sentence is *hallowed*. The definition here is not to "be made holy," for God's name is already holy. It is already set apart, regardless of whether we pray for it to be or not. As one scholar explains it, the meaning of *hallowed* in the Model Prayer is to "be *counted* holy."[22] We should pray that what God reveals about himself would be acknowledged and revered by others. After all, his name is the one supreme standard of truth for us and a means of knowing God and approaching him. Therefore, his name *deserves* to be counted as holy!

Where It's Placed

The Model Prayer begins with "Our Father who is in heaven," and it is immediately followed by "Hallowed be your name." That order is hugely significant. We are not really ready to praise God unless we have first acknowledged him as high and lifted up.

In 1 Kings 8:27 Solomon said to God, "The heavens, even the highest heaven, cannot contain you." The Lord asked Jeremiah, "Do I not fill the heavens and the earth?" (Jeremiah 23:24). From that we see that God isn't restricted to one location. He is omnipresent. Yet, in the Model Prayer, Jesus instructed us to pray to our Father who is in *heaven*. Have you ever stopped to think why he would do that? Why not say, "Our Father who is everywhere"? That is certainly a true statement, so why specify the Father's location as heaven?

Heaven is where God's throne is. Psalm 113:4-6 says, "The Lord is high above all nations; His glory is above the heavens. Who is like the Lord our God, Who is enthroned on high?" Isaiah writes, "Thus says the Lord, 'Heaven is My throne and the earth is My footstool'" (66:1). In the Model Prayer, I believe Jesus was instructing us to *focus* on the Father who is high and lifted up above all the earth. Setting our minds on things above helps prepare us for praise and to respond to him in true worship.

There are many passages encouraging us to think above this world and ourselves and focus on the Lord in glory. Revelation 4:1-3 is a great example. Please read that now. Is there anything about this passage that is especially encouraging to you?

What if John had not been invited to "come up here" to see a vision of heaven? Would he have seen the throne from down below where he was? More importantly, would John have realized that Someone was *sitting* on that throne? Probably not. Who did John see on the throne? He saw God. John didn't see him that day sitting there wringing his hands, worried about what was going to happen. He is the Most High over all the earth. He is in control. What a revelation John had! What a life-altering moment that must have been for John. And it was because he *looked up*.

"Hallowed be your name" is a wonderful expression of praise, and it's so fitting and well-placed at this early point in the Model Prayer. Once we've focused on God as our Father, once we've taken time to really lift our mind and thoughts above the stuff around us, and once we place our attention on the true and living God and recognize he's on the throne of glory, then it's time to offer a sacrifice of praise to him.

Stop now and focus your mind. Imagine God sitting on the throne. Don't try to see what he looks like or how glorious he is, for that is impossible to do. Try to imagine a bigger-than-life figure you know to be God sitting on a bigger-than-life throne. Go ahead; focus your thoughts on that for a moment. As you think on his greatness and majesty, what do you want to say to God? How do you want to connect with him right now? I'm guessing you would like to pour out some praise to him, maybe tell him you love him and express your gratitude and awe to him somehow. After all, that is the most natural and appropriate thing to do. Don't rush this moment. Give praise to his most awesome, *hallowed* name!

Here are three important take-aways from today's lesson.

- First, our praise should be *actual*. We need to actually praise the Lord. It's not enough to think about praising God, and it doesn't matter whether we "feel" like praising him. He's always worthy of our worship. We should choose to praise him every day.
- Also, our praise should be *accurate*. What Jesus prayed—that God's name be acknowledged as holy—was a precise statement supported by Scripture. For our praise to be acceptable to the Lord, it must be based on what the Bible says about God.
- Finally, our praise should be *authentic*. We should not only "talk" our praise; we should walk it every day. If we mean those words to let his name be hallowed, and if we really want his name to be counted as holy on this earth, then we need to live and act as though his name is holy. We need to live a life set apart for his honor and glory.

Abraham is a great example of someone whose praise was authentic. Everywhere Abraham went, he built an altar of worship to God. When he went into Canaan, a Canaanite passing by observed they had a new neighbor, for he had seen Abraham's altar. When Abraham began doing business with the Canaanites, they found him to be honest. Everything he said strengthened their confidence in him. That led them to conclude that the God whom Abraham worshiped was indeed a holy God. The king of the Philistines even said to him, "God is obviously with you, helping you in everything you do" (Genesis 21:22). To quote Dr. J. Vernon McGee, "The entire life of Abraham revealed the reverence he felt for God. Surely the name of God was made holy in Canaan because of Abraham."[23]

Praying the Prayer

To let us better praise God's name, we need to study it. In his book, *Exalt His Name*, Dr. Vernon Whaley explains that there are actually fourteen formal names which identify God's character and purpose in the Old Testament.[24] I've listed those below. I've included brief definitions for the names along with verses that contain each name.

Please carefully read through the list; then choose one or two names to thank God for right now. Journal your prayer of praise. Also consider kneeling as you pray, if you are physically able.

- *Elohim* means God, Mighty Creator, or Judge. "In the beginning, God [Elohim] created the heavens and the earth" (Genesis 1:1).

- *El Elyon* means "Most High" or "the Highest." God's sovereignty and majesty are revealed and held in highest, exalted authority. "I cry out to God Most High [El Elyon], to God who will fulfill his purpose for me" (Psalm 57:2).
- *El Roi* means "the God who sees" and knows everything about us—our past, present and future. "The LORD [El Roi] keeps watch over you as you come and go, both now and forever" (Psalm 121:8).
- *El Shaddai*, the Covenant name of God, means God Almighty. It stresses God's ability to completely nourish, satisfy, supply and sustain those he loves. "Those who live in the shelter of the Most High will find rest in the shadow of the Almighty. This I declare about the LORD [El Shaddai]: He alone is my refuge, my place of safety; he is my God, and I trust him" (Psalm 91:1-2).
- *El Olam* means The Everlasting God, The God of Eternity, The God of the Universe, The God of Ancient Days. "But the LORD [El Olam] is the only true God. He is the living God and the everlasting King! The whole earth trembles at his anger. The nations cannot stand up to his wrath" (Jeremiah 10:10).
- *Yahweh*, or Jehovah, means Lord and declares God as absolute, independent, self-existent, the source of all life without beginning or end, the 'I AM WHO I AM.' "The name of the LORD [Yahweh] is a strong fortress; the godly run to him and are safe" (Proverbs 18:10).
- *Adonai* means Lord, Master, Provider or Owner, the one who possesses all things. "'I am commander of the LORD's [Adonai's] army.' At this, Joshua fell with his face to the ground in reverence. 'I am at your command,' Joshua said. 'What do you want your servant to do?'" (Joshua 5:14).
- *Jehovah Jireh* means The Lord, our Provider. "Abraham named the place Yahweh-Yireh (which means 'the LORD will provide'). To this day, people still use that name as a proverb: 'On the mountain of the LORD [Jehovah Jireh] it will be provided'" (Genesis 22:14).
- *Jehovah Rophe* means The Lord Who heals or makes healthy. "Bless the LORD, O my soul, and all that is within me, bless his holy name! Bless the LORD [Jehovah Rophe], O my soul, and forget not all his benefits, who forgives all your iniquity, who heals all your diseases" (Psalm 103:2-3).

- *Jehovah Nissi* means The Lord, my Banner of victory, my refuge, my strength, my miracle. "And Moses built an altar and named it The LORD [Jehovah Nissi] Is My Banner" (Exodus 17:15).
- *Jehovah Shalom* means The Lord is my Peace. "And Gideon built an altar to the LORD [Jehovah Shalom] there and named it Yahweh-Shalom (which means 'the LORD is peace')" (Judges 6:24).
- *Jehovah Raah* means The Lord is my Shepherd. "The LORD [Jehovah Raah] is my shepherd; I have all that I need" (Psalm 23:1).
- *Jehovah Tsidkenu* means The Lord our Righteousness. "And this will be his name: 'The LORD [Jehovah Tsidkenu] Is Our Righteousness.' In that day Judah will be saved, and Israel will live in safety" (Jeremiah 23:6).
- *Jehovah Shammah* means The Lord is there and ever present. "The distance around the entire city will be 6 miles. And from that day the name of the city will be 'The LORD [Jehovah Shammah] Is There'" (Ezekiel 48:35).

Living the Prayer

You've focused your thoughts on your Father in Heaven and praised his hallowed name—the HE part of the prayer model. Now take a few moments to pray for your own needs (WE) and for the needs of others (THEY). Do you have a burden that only El Roi knows about? Ask him to watch over you today! Is a close friend or family member ill? Petition Jehovah Rophe for healing! Are missionaries you're praying for facing adversity or persecution? Entreat Jehovah Nissi to go before them as their banner of victory! Do you know of an urgent need in your community or church that just isn't being met? Go to Jehovah Jireh and ask him to provide (and don't be surprised if he reveals how you can be his agent in that provision)! Be sure to journal about what and whom you pray for.

JOURNAL

DAY 5: *YOUR WILL*

Let's start off today reciting the HE section of the prayer model. Say it out loud if you can. "Our Father which art in heaven, Hallowed be thy name. Thy kingdom come. Thy will be done in earth, as it is in heaven."

⟲ Say those last two sentences again slowly: "Thy kingdom come. Thy will be done in earth, as it is in heaven." Now say them one more time as a prayer to God.

In his book, *The Kingdom of God*, Dr. Martin Lloyd-Jones explains God's kingdom like this: "It is the rule of God, it is the reign of God. It means the coming of righteousness, the coming of peace. It means that evil is controlled and defeated; it means that God's blessings are showered upon the Christian. It means that we bask in the sunshine of God's favour."[25] That is some powerful incentive to pray for his kingdom to come!

We're going to deal a lot more with the kingdom of God in the weeks to come. There is definitely much to learn and great depths of truth to apply. But for now, here is what we need to understand about the kingdom:

It's not yours.

Let me say that again: It is not your kingdom.

It is God's.

⟲ How does that strike you? Does that idea bother you a little down deep inside? Does it elate you? Are you okay asking for *God's* kingdom to come rather than your own?

We'll also delve deeper into the will of God as we progress in the study. Again, there is much to discover and apply. But for now, this is what we need to realize about the will of God:

It is not your will.

It's his.

It is his will that matters.

In the first part of the Model Prayer, we do not pray for our will to be done. We are asking for God's will to be accomplished, to be followed, to be submitted to. It is *his* will that should be done, period. We are praying for his kingdom to come in its fullness so that all created beings may bring their wills into harmony with God's will.

So you see, it literally has nothing to do with our will. Before we are ready to move to the next part of the Model Prayer, we must first understand what it means to die to our selfish attitudes and wants.

♫	Savor these passages now. Meditate on them.

"My old self has been crucified with Christ. It is no longer I who live, but Christ lives in me. So I live in this earthly body by trusting in the Son of God, who loved me and gave himself for me" (Galatians 2:20 NLT).

"Then Jesus said to his disciples, "If any of you wants to be my follower, you must give up your own way, take up your cross, and follow me. If you try to hang on to your life, you will lose it. But if you give up your life for my sake, you will save it" (Matthew 16:24-25 NLT).

"Father, if you are willing, please take this cup of suffering away from me. Yet I want your will to be done, not mine" (Luke 22:42 NLT).

"Your will be done, on earth as it is in heaven" (Matthew 6:9 ESV).

Surrender

In regards to praying for God's kingdom to come, Dr. Lloyd-Jones writes, "You make an obvious total surrender, you cast yourself entirely into His hands. You deny yourself, you take up your cross and you follow Him and if you do these things, the kingdom of God is within you. You have entered the kingdom and the kingdom has entered you…"[26]

It's worth saying again: It is not about your will or mine. It is his will we should be praying would be accomplished. Praying for the Lord's will to be done necessitates that we first *surrender* our own will and wants.

♫	This might be a really good time to stop and evaluate where you are with his will versus your own. To help, I encourage you to do what I call a "wants check."

1. First, jot down everything you can think of that you *want*. These can be hopes, plans, objects, people, money, jobs, whatever. Write down what comes to your mind. Don't filter them. Some may be "guilty pleasures" you would rather not admit or put onto paper. But do it anyway. Write down every wish and want inside of you—the good, the bad, and the ugly. Don't rush through this exercise. Be thorough, and by all means, be honest.

2. Now, look closely at your list of wants. Walk through each item. Ask yourself: "Is this something that could bring God glory

or do I mainly want it for myself?" Place a mark beside any desires that you suspect could have selfish or ungodly motives.

3. Finally, ask the Lord to give you discernment about the "wants" you are unsure of. Be intentional with each one. Call it out before God and say, "Lord, I surrender this desire to you. If this is something you want for me, please help me patiently wait for it. If it is not your will for me to have it, help me turn away from it and no longer chase after it."

Yourself

You may have noticed there are more references to you in this lesson than we normally include. I prefer to say "we" and include myself as often as possible as we go through this study together. However, today this *is* about you. I can't help to soften the blow for you. This lesson is between you and God. The laser of truth is focused on *your* heart. Each of us must examine our own selves before the Lord. And this is your time to do that.

The incredible truth is that the Lord knows about your issues and imperfections and he loves you anyway! In Psalm 103 David wrote, "He has removed our sins as far from us as the east is from the west. The LORD is like a father to his children, tender and compassionate to those who fear him. For he knows how weak we are; he remembers we are only dust" (verses 12-14). Hallelujah!

The Lord has compassion on us and patience with us as his dearly loved children. And even more than that, he places in us the *will* to do his good pleasure. How awesome is that? As the New Living Translation puts it: "For God is working in you, giving you the desire and the power to do what pleases him" (Philippians 2:13).

If you are struggling to let go of some things in your life and fully surrender, don't beat yourself up or be impatient with your progress. He is cheering for you and determined to shape you into his image. He loves you just the way you are! Like the children's song says...

> He's still working on me
> To make me what I need to be
> It took him just a week to make the moon and stars
> The sun and the earth and Jupiter and Mars
> How loving and patient he must be
> 'Cause he's still workin' on me [27]

Read Psalm 139. Read it slowly to catch every word. Now write out verses 23 and 24 in your own words, making them your personal prayer to God.

JOURNAL

Praying the Prayer

If the Lord has exposed some sins or wrong attitudes hidden away in your heart today, take time now to confess those individually to him. Trust him to forgive you and cleanse you from all unrighteousness, as 1 John 1:9 promises he will!

Pray through each part of the prayer model. Make this a powerful time of communion with your Father as you move from HE to WE to THEY. Be sure to journal about what and whom you pray for.

HE – Vertical

JOURNAL

WE – Personal
Seek your Abba's help with meeting your needs and the needs of those you love. Perhaps you can think of someone close to you who desperately needs to know God as his or her Abba Father and could focus on that person today.

THEY – Kingdom

This is your time to pray for people and about situations outside your immediate realm of concern. Who would benefit by having a relationship with our Abba Father? What situation in your world, nation, state, or church would benefit from the intervention of our Almighty God?

Read (or better yet sing!) the old hymn below as a prayer to God. Remind yourself of it several times as you go through your day. Also, pick one of the verses mentioned in this lesson to meditate on over the next few days.

All to Jesus I surrender
All to Him I freely give
I will ever love and trust Him
In His presence daily live

All to Jesus I surrender
Humbly at His feet I bow
Worldly pleasures all forsaken
Take me Jesus take me now

All to Jesus I surrender
Lord I give myself to Thee
Fill me with Thy love and power
Let Thy blessings fall on me

I surrender all
I surrender all
All to Thee my blessed Savior
I surrender all [28]

WEEK 2 FOLLOW-UP QUESTIONS FOR GROUP DISCUSSION

1. In Day 1 we learned there was a paradigm shift between the way Old Testament believers viewed God and how Jesus encouraged his followers to view God. Which perspective reflects your own relationship with him? Can you explain why you're inclined to see God that way?
2. How does it make you feel to be called a child of God?
3. How is addressing God as "Jehovah" (Lord—the absolute independent, self-existent source of all life) or "Elohim" (Mighty Creator or Judge) different from calling him "Abba" (Papa or Daddy)?
4. How does it make you feel to be able—to have the right as a beloved adopted child—to call Jehovah God "Papa"?
5. Reread Revelation 1:9-18. How would you have reacted if you had encountered Christ as John did?
6. Why is it important to think of God as both "our Father who is exalted above all else" and our gracious, loving Abba?
7. What does it mean to "enter [God's] gates with thanksgiving and his courts with praise" (Psalm 100:4 NIV)? Why is this practice important?
8. The names of God reflect his character. Which names resonate most with you? In other words, which names reflect aspects of his character that you're most grateful for?
9. Why is it important to be very clear that the kingdom and the will mentioned in the Model Prayer are not our kingdom and not our will?
10. In Matthew 16:24, Jesus tells his disciples, "Whoever wants to be my disciple must deny themselves and take up their cross and follow me" (NIV). What would it look like in today's world to do that?

Footnotes for Week 2:

[1] S.M. Lockridge, quote from "He's My King" sermon preached in 1976, http://www.youtube.com/watch?v=4BhI4JKACUs.

[2] C.H. Spurgeon, *"Our Father Which Art in Heaven,"* delivered on September 12, 1858 at the Music Hall, Royal Surrey Gardens, https://www.blueletterbible.org/Comm/spurgeon_charles/sermons/0213.cfm.

[3] *ibid.*

[4] J.I. Packer, *Knowing God* (Illinois: Intervarsity Press, 1973), 201.

[5] Strong's Concordance, "5. Abba," *Bible Hub,* https://biblehub.com/greek/5.htm.

[6] Strong's Concordance, "3962. patér," *Bible Hub,* https://biblehub.com/greek/5.htm.

[7] Dennis L. Okholm, "Prayer," *Bible Study Tools,* https://www.biblestudytools.com/dictionary/prayer.

[8] *ibid.*

[9] C.H. Spurgeon, *"Our Father Which Art in Heaven,"* delivered on September 12, 1858 at the Music Hall, Royal Surrey Gardens, https://www.blueletterbible.org/Comm/spurgeon_charles/sermons/0213.cfm.

[10] Tony Brown and Pat Barrett, *Good, Good Father,* Barrett Daddy Music/Capitol CMG Paragon/Common Hymnal Digital/Housefires Sounds/Lion's Den Family Music/Sixsteps Music/Tony Brown Publishing Designee (Capitol)/Vamos Publishing/Worshiptogether.com Songs/WORSHIPTOGETHER.Com Songs, 2014.

[11] Charles Swindoll, *Intimacy with the Almighty* (Dallas: Word, 1996), 4.

[12] Matthew James Redman and Beth Louise Redman, *Let My Words Be Few*, Meadowgreen Music Company, Thank You Music Ltd., 2003.

[13] J.I. Packer, *Knowing God* (Illinois: Intervarsity Press, 1973), 203.

[14] Robert H. Stein, "Fatherhood of God," *Bible Study Tools*, https://www.biblestudytools.com/dictionaries/bakers-evangelical-dictionary/fatherhood-of-god.html.

[15] Dr. Herb Armentrout, from teaching on "Worship Basics" at a NLW Community Gathering, April 23, 2020.

[16] Jamieson-Fausset-Brown Bible Commentary, "Matthew 6:9," *Bible Hub*, https://biblehub.com/commentaries/matthew/6-9.htm.

[17] J.I. Packer, *Praying the Lord's Prayer* (Wheaton, Illinois: Crossway, 2007), 35, 37.

[18] Max Lucado, *Fearless* (Nashville: Thomas Nelson, 2009), 169.

[19] C.S Lewis, *Prince Caspian* (New York: Harper Collins, 1951), 79.

[20] Vernon Whaley, *Exalt His Name: Understanding Music and Worship* (Illinois: Evangelical Training Association, 2017), 101-102.

[21] Pulpit Commentary, "Matthew 6:9," *Bible Hub,* https://biblehub.com/matthew/6-9.htm.

[22] *ibid.*

[23] J. Vernon McGee, *Thru the Bible* (Nashville: Thomas Nelson, 1981), Volume IV, p. 37.

[24] *Exalt His Name,* 102-113.

[25] Martin Lloyd-Jones, *The Kingdom of God* (Wheaton, Illinois: Crossway, 1992), 21.

[26] *ibid,* p. 66.

[27] Joel Hemphill, *He's Still Working on Me,* Universal Music Publishing Group, 1980.

[28] Judson W. Van DeVenter, *I Surrender All*, 1896.

WEEK 3 PERSONAL PRAYER

Give us this day our daily bread. And forgive us our debts,
as we forgive our debtors. And lead us not into temptation,
but deliver us from evil.
Matthew 6:11-13a KJV

DAY 1 *ON EARTH*

Welcome to Week 3! I believe this week of study can be a huge encouragement to you. I am convinced we will be less burdened and more hopeful and peaceful after we have gone through these next five lessons.

We have explored the HE or vertical part of the Model Prayer. Now we are ready to examine the WE section, which is the personal part of the Model Prayer. It is here that we can let go of our anxieties, tell God what we need and thank him for all he has done. When we do, his Word promises we will experience God's peace, which exceeds anything we can understand (Philippians 4:7).

It's not reasonable, though, to think that everything we study will be uplifting and encouraging. This book is about *living* the Model Prayer. Our goal is to put into practice in our daily lives the truths and principles we discover within this prayer. Therefore, we may face some realities which cause us to have to rethink—even *change*—how we pray and live. (And change isn't something most people like to do!)

⸘ Please pause now and pray. Thank God for this time in his Word. Ask him to teach you and correct you if needed this week. Surrender yourself afresh to his will.

Backdrop
When we pray, "Your kingdom come; Your will be done," what are we

really saying? Have you ever thought about that? Whether we realize it or not, we are stating a powerful reality. Every time we quote that part of the prayer, we are acknowledging that God's kingdom has not fully come. Else, why would Jesus include that petition within his prayer model? I think we can all agree we are not living in anything close to the utopia of heaven. As my grandaddy used to say, "This ain't it." As far as our eyes can observe, God's will is not being done "on earth as it is in heaven."

There was a time when God's perfect will *was* being played out on the earth. The world was a utopia. When God created it, the earth was perfect for Adam and Eve. Unfortunately, they blew it. God, in his ultimate wisdom, gave them a will of their own, and they willfully chose to sin, to go against what God had instructed them. At that moment, their utopian lifestyle was over. They got kicked out of the Garden. They became mere mortals that day, and all of creation was set on a vicious course of decay and death.

We have the same sinful nature in us that Adam and Eve had. As Romans 5:12 says, "When Adam sinned, sin entered the world. Adam's sin brought death, so death spread to everyone, for everyone sinned." We also have the same opportunity that Adam and Eve had, to choose for ourselves. We have a *will*. We have our own ideas and ways of doing things. As a friend of mine said to me: In heaven God's will has no competition, but on earth, there are many wills vying for dominance. There is our will. There is Satan's will. There is the will of every person on this earth—many of whom are trying to impose it on us.

Bottom line is that we live in a fallen world where God's kingdom still has not come and his will is not always done. That harsh reality colors everything we will talk about this week. We can't ignore that truth. We cannot blow past the first part of the Lord's Prayer and miss the need to pray that his kingdom come on earth. Understanding and embracing this often overlooked reality can help us know how and for what we should pray. It can help us to better pray and experience the personal section of the prayer model.

Perspective
Some people approach the WE portion of the Lord's Prayer as an opportunity to "name and claim" anything they ask for. But that doesn't really work in a world where so many don't follow Jesus. If we've surrendered our lives to Christ, God's kingdom has come into our hearts.

But lamentably, not everybody around us has done that. Not everyone knows and loves the Lord as we do. We still live in a filthy, fallen world.

Isaiah acknowledged this. He writes, "Woe is me! For I am lost; for I am a man of unclean lips, and I dwell in the midst of a people of unclean lips; for my eyes have seen the King, the LORD of hosts!" (Isaiah 6:5b ESV). He saw beyond himself. Even though he confessed and was cleansed of his own sin, he still realized he lived among people who were unclean. He had the proper perspective. He saw himself as part of a bigger picture, and that's how we should see ourselves as well.

Although we are not to follow this world, we are still *in* it. When Jesus prayed for us in John 17, he said to his Father, "I am not asking that You take them out of the world, but that You keep them from the evil one...As You sent Me into the world, I have also sent them into the world" (verses 15, 18). We should earnestly and often pray that God's kingdom will come to this earth and his will be done here. Why? Because this is where God has sent us to be salt and light.

Things can seem hopeless and hard down here at times. We may be tempted to just give up on this 'ole world and focus our attention on the "sweet by and by." But we don't have that option. We are on a mission, as Jesus was, "to seek and to save those who are lost" (Luke 19:10). We should intercede on behalf of the people Christ died for. In doing so, we are helping expand his kingdom here on earth.

Encounter

As we have seen, Paul says in Colossians 3 to set our minds on things above, not on things on earth. Yet, Paul didn't live life with his head in the clouds. His feet were on the ground where people are. While he longed to go and be with Christ, "which would be far better for me," still he writes, "for your sakes, it is better that I continue to live" (Philippians 1:23b-24). Like Isaiah, Paul saw the bigger picture. He knew God had called him to serve others and place their needs above his own comforts.

In chapter 16 of Acts, Paul and Silas had a heavenly encounter in a very earthly place. In a real sense, heaven touched earth inside a stinking prison. Go to Acts 16:16-38 now. This is quite a bit of reading, but it is needed to get the full impact of this fascinating story. As you read, notice how Paul and Silas represented the Lord in this story. How did they put others' needs in front of their own?

Here are some ways I believe Paul and Silas brought heaven to earth.

Praising. Verse 25 says, "Around midnight Paul and Silas were praying and singing hymns to God, and the other prisoners were listening." What a great example of heaven being brought to earth! Psalm 22:3 says God is enthroned on praise. He dwells in it! In my first book, *Pure Praise: A Heart-focused Bible Study on Worship*, I talk at length about the priority of praise. "At this very moment in heaven, God is being praised...Praise to our holy God is so important that heaven itself never stops praising him."[1] There was a loud roar of praise to the Lord in heaven at the exact moment Paul and Silas were *praising* him in that jail cell!

Preaching. An earthquake hit and the prisoners' chains fell off and the prison doors flew open. The jailer was ready to kill himself. But when he realized none had escaped, he brought out Paul and Silas and asked, "Sirs, what must I do to be saved?" They shared the word of the Lord with him and with all who lived in his household. What better way to bring heaven to earth than by *preaching* the gospel to those who are lost?

Partying. The jailer's entire family placed their trust in Christ and were baptized that very night. Talk about a reason to rejoice! Can you imagine how much excitement and tears of joy there must have been? What greater way to celebrate than by enjoying a good meal together? Jesus once said, "There is joy in the presence of God's angels when even one sinner repents" (Luke 15:10). As Paul and Silas and that family feasted together, heaven was *partying* with them.

Putting things right. Rather than getting out of town that night, Paul and Silas remained in the custody of the jailer. The next morning the police came and told them they were free to go. But Paul replied, "They have publicly beaten us without a trial and put us in prison—and we are Roman citizens. So now they want us to leave secretly? Certainly not! Let them come themselves to release us!" Paul wasn't content to just sweep this incident under the carpet. He held the officials' feet to the fire. *Putting things right* was important to Paul. This was a very serious offense on the part of the magistrates. Paul wanted a public apology, and he got it. As N.T. Wright explains, "This is what the kingdom of God looks like when it's on the road, arriving on earth as in heaven."[2]

Trouble

Jesus told his disciples, "In the world you will have tribulation. But take heart; I have overcome the world" (John 16:33b ESV). Quoting Dr. Wright again, "The kingdom will come as the church, energized by the Spirit, goes out into the world vulnerable, suffering, praising, praying, misunderstood, misjudged, vindicated, celebrating…so that the life of Jesus may also be manifest."[3]

When we live out the Model Prayer in our daily lives, when we seek to help bring heaven to earth, we will rub some people the wrong way. We will annoy people, and they may give us resistance. For God to be glorified and his will to be done, we may even have to endure some suffering along the way.

A good example of one who has endured suffering in order for God to be glorified is a young Pakistani woman named Tara. She grew up in a prominent and strict Muslim home. When she was 12, she secretly ordered a Bible correspondence course. When she was 16, she secretly attended a Christian church service. And when she was 17, in the privacy of her bedroom, she called on Emmanuel to save her. When her father and brother found out, they beat her severely and threatened to kill her if she stopped being a Muslim. She was forced to run away from home and go into hiding. But Tara grew strong in her faith. She became a powerful witness in Pakistan. Many have turned to Christ because of her love and devotion to him. She has not denied her faith, even though it could one day cost her her life.

Why is Tara so bold in her stand? Why risk pain and death? Something she said when she was 18 might shed light on that for us. Tara wanted to go out evangelizing on the streets of Pakistan, and a friend expressed concerned for her. "Rubin," she said to him, "what is more important, my safety or the lost souls we're trying to reach?"[4] Tara was willing to endure suffering to help bring people into God's kingdom, to help his will be done on earth.

The most incredible example of suffering that led to God's will being done is Jesus dying on the cross for our salvation. Slowly read Matthew 26:36-46. Imagine yourself in that scene with Jesus. Try to empathize with the agony he felt. What if Jesus had not yielded to his Father's will in that moment? What impact could his omission have had on you and your outlook on life?

For God's kingdom to come in our hearts and ultimately on the earth, Christ had to die for our sins. In order to accomplish God's will and finish his plan of redemption for mankind, Jesus had to go through horrific suffering. Or to put it another way, "Because of the joy awaiting him, he endured the cross, disregarding its shame. Now he is seated in the place of honor beside God's throne" (Hebrews 12:2b).

Jesus lived his whole life to please his Father. He himself said his nourishment came "from doing the will of God...from finishing his work" (John 4:34). When we take up our cross to follow him, we too relinquish all rights to comfort and instant gratification. What Paul writes in 2 Corinthians could become our testimony as well: "Through suffering, our bodies continue to share in the death of Jesus so that the life of Jesus may also be seen in our bodies" (4:10).

Praying the Prayer

Journal each section of the Model Prayer again today. Please take your time and be sure what you write comes from a heart that longs to worship the Lord.

HE – Vertical
The worship song "Honestly," by Carl Cartee, expresses the need to surrender oneself to the advancement of God's kingdom on earth:

> If I leave behind all that's familiar,
> Could I do what has never been done?
> If I believed in you like You believe in me,
> Could I finish the work you've begun?
> Honestly I need to be broken
> And honestly I need to fall down.
> Go ahead and shake my foundations
> Cause honestly I'm figuring out
> That of all that I have,
> All that I need is you.
> Honestly.[5]

Journal your words of commitment today as you worship the One whose "soul was overwhelmed with sorrow" as he honestly contemplated his death on the cross (Matthew 26:38).

JOURNAL

WE – Personal

Record some things that concern you right now, maybe a family issue or feelings of inadequacy that interfere with your commitment to continue the work of Christ. Tell Jehovah Raah, your Shepherd, what your needs are.

JOURNAL

THEY – Kingdom

Ask God to reveal your role in advancing his kingdom outside your immediate sphere of interest. Pray for the situations that prevent others from being part of his kingdom.

Living the Prayer

In the past when you've prayed, "Your kingdom come, your will be done," did you realize what you were actually praying and what you might be getting yourself into? You might need to experience some hardships, and suffering might need to happen in order for you to finish the work the Lord has for you and for him to get the most glory from your life. Journal an honest response to God now. Express how you feel about what he has shown you today.

DAY 2: *GIVE US*

There is a well-known verse in James 4 that says, "You have not because you ask not" (v. 2). Or put another way, you don't have something because you don't ask for it. R.A. Torrey writes, "These words contain the secret of the poverty and powerlessness of the average Christian—neglect of prayer."[6] God expects us to ask for the things we need. There is a cause and effect involved with prayer. We pray; he answers. If we don't pray, he doesn't answer. Simple as that.

Today we come to the second part of the Model Prayer—the WE section—where we get to turn our attention toward things we need. This part is very personal and bold as we lay our petitions before the Lord. God enjoys giving his children things we need. He loves to hear and answer our prayers. In Psalm 18, David writes, "I cried to my God for help. From his temple he heard my voice; my cry came before him, into his ears" (v. 6 NIV). First John chapter 5 reads, "And we are confident that he hears us whenever we ask for anything that pleases him. And since we know he hears us when we make our requests, we also know that he will give us what we ask for" (v. 14-15).

So, what do you need right now? What is something you'd like to ask God for? Please write that in the space below, so you can see it in black and white in front of you. We'll return to this need throughout the lesson.

JOURNAL

When we ask God for something there are 3 questions we need to consider:

Is He Able?
Go back to the need you just wrote down. Do you believe God is able to handle that need for you? Can he do it? Does he have the power and wealth and wisdom to pull it off? Can you trust him with that request?

Believing God is able is a deeply spiritual thing. It is not sufficient to believe it in our minds; we must accept it down deep in our hearts. We can't wrap our minds around the hugeness of God, nor can we possibly figure him out with mere brainpower alone. Listen to what God said to Israel: "My thoughts are nothing like your thoughts...And my ways are far beyond anything you could imagine. For just as the heavens are higher than the earth, so my ways are higher than your ways and my thoughts higher than your thoughts" (Isaiah 55:8-9). No wonder Paul wrote, "O, the depth of the riches of the wisdom and knowledge of God! How unsearchable are His judgments, and untraceable His ways! 'Who has known the mind of the Lord? Or who has been His counselor?'" (Romans 11:8-9 NIV).

So again, I ask you, *is he able*? It is vitally important that we believe that he is, as we approach him with our requests. Here's why: "...without faith it is impossible to please Him, for he who comes to God must believe that He is [God], and that He is a rewarder of those who diligently seek Him" (Hebrews 11:6 NKJ). We must believe he is in fact the true and living God, the God who made the entire universe. Do you believe that *that* God is able?

Is He Willing?

This question shrinks the number of possibilities of appropriate requests quite a bit. After all, God is able to do anything. But that does not mean he is *willing* to do anything. For example, a person might want someone else's spouse for him or herself. But no matter how much a person prays and asks for it, God will not grant that wish. Don't even bother to ask for stuff that is clearly outside his precepts and revealed will. We must ask for things that are *within* the parameters of his written Word, the Bible. Prayer is not a genie in a bottle.

If our request doesn't qualify as acceptable to God, then we can't "faith" it into existence—no matter how spiritual we think we are or how much we try to muster belief that he is able to answer it. The answer to the question "Is he willing?" is more intellectual in nature. It is a matter of doctrine, so it requires that we think. Thus, we had better dig into the Bible and see if he even allows for our particular request. We must search the Scriptures and do our "best to present ourselves to God as one approved, correctly handling the Word of Truth" (2 Timothy 2:15b).

The kind of prayers we can be assured he loves to answer are those that bring him glory and build up his kingdom. Jesus made some startling promises in John 15 about that. Please take time to read verses 7-8 and verse 16 now. According to this passage, how crucial is it that your prayer requests bring God glory and bear much fruit? How important do you think these things are to God and to his answering our requests?

🜉 Look at your prayer need again, the one you wrote out earlier in this lesson. Does it go against any laws or principles God gave in his Word? Also, if he granted this request could it bring glory to him in some way?

Will He Do It?

This third question is more practical and individual in nature. Even though God is able and may be willing to do something, it doesn't guarantee he will do that "something" for you or me. Whether he grants our requests may simply come down to how determined we are to *ask* in faith and in humility.

Jesus says in his Sermon on the Mount to "Keep on asking, and you will receive what you ask for. Keep on seeking, and you will find. Keep on knocking, and the door will be opened to you" (Matthew 7:7 NLT). Unfortunately many give up and quit praying after only a short time of asking. They grow impatient or lose faith that God will answer. We need to be like the widow in the parable in Luke 18, who kept coming to the judge demanding justice for a dispute. The judge finally gave in. He said, "This woman is driving me crazy. I'm going to see that she gets justice, because she is wearing me out with her constant requests!" (verse 5 NLT).

Of course, we could never wear God out or "drive him crazy." He loves us and wants us to come to him again and again. One might wonder though how long we should keep on asking. The answer: Until we get a response. For some it may be days, and for others it might be months or even years before God answers. But answer he will *if* we keep praying until we pray through. As I heard a pastor say, *praying through* is all about consistency. It is "circling Jericho" until God tells you to stop.

Case Study

Let's put these questions to the test now with a familiar request that is in the Lord's Prayer: "Give us this day our daily bread."

First, is God *able* to give us what we need each day? The obvious answer is a resounding yes! If he could send the Israelites manna from heaven each day for 40 years while they wandered out in the middle of nowhere, then he can certainly send us whatever we need when we need it, no matter where we are. Since Jesus could feed 5000-plus people with only

5 loaves of bread and 2 fishes (and have 12 baskets of food left over!) we can be assured he can take our little and make it more than enough.

Second, is God *willing* to give us what we need each day? I think you should see this answer for yourself straight from his written Word.

ॐ   Please read Matthew 7:7-11 now. Underline anything you see in this amazing passage that shows evidence that the Father wants to give to us.

When I was growing up I had a dog named Rascal. I loved to take him around to my neighborhood friends and prove how much stronger and better Rascal was than their dogs. One of my favorite things was to show them how high he could jump. I would hold a treat above him, and he would jump up to try and get it. But as he jumped I would move my hand so he couldn't quite reach it. The higher I lifted the biscuit, the higher he jumped.

I believe we think God handles us as I did Rascal, that somehow, we must jump as high as we possibly can and work hard to earn his provision and love. But that is not at all true. If we really need something, all we have to do is ask, and he will bring it right down to where we are when we need it. He is more than willing to meet our every need, because he is our awesome and eternal Father.

ॐ   Finally, will God *actually give* you the bread you need and are requesting? Ask yourself: Are you his child? Are you in the family of God because you've been born again? Are you seeking the kingdom of God above all else and living righteously? If so, Jesus himself promised he will give you everything you need (Matthew 6:33). You and I don't need some special revelation to know this. This is a promise for each and every blood-bought Christian. Millions of saints who've gone before us have tried and proven this time and time again.

Take-aways

What should we ask for? There are 3 take-aways we need to learn from this request in the Model Prayer:

It is a *present* request. We are to pray, "Give us *this day*..." Jesus wasn't saying we should not plan ahead. We should think ahead and plan as much as we can. However, we should never worry about the future. Jesus said, "So don't worry about these things, saying, 'What will we eat? What will we drink? What will we wear?' These things dominate the thoughts of unbelievers, but your heavenly Father already knows all your needs...

So don't worry about tomorrow, for tomorrow will bring its own worries. Today's trouble is enough for today" (Matthew 6:31-32, 34).

It's a *particular* request. "Give us this day our *daily bread*." That's quite specific. What do you really need? List your needs as specifically as you can. Write them down in a journal. Then, when God answers and provides, be sure to share it with others so they too can praise God for his faithfulness!

It's a *practical* request. "Give us this day our daily *bread*." Bread was a common dietary staple back then. Growing up I was spoiled to a huge three-course meal three times a day. However, as I've gotten older I realize I don't need near that much food. Whether it is food or clothing or finances or something else, we need to ask ourselves, "What do we really need?" Does God only want you to eat bread? Should we never ask for anything else? Absolutely not! God loves to bless his children. But we should minimize seeking after unnecessary things. Pray for what you need; then watch him bless you beyond that. Remember what Jesus said in Matthew 7: "How much more will your heavenly Father give to those who ask?" (verse 11). Our Father is a "much more" God!

When to Stop Asking

Before we close I want us to consider one more thing. What if the "answer" God gives to our request isn't exactly what we expected or prayed for? What should we do then? I think Paul's account of his thorn in the flesh can shed some light on that for us.

Please read 2 Corinthians 12:5-10. Look closely at what God said to Paul. What word is surprisingly absent from his reply?

The word that is missing, the one word I used to assume God had said, is "no." But God never actually told Paul no. Here's another startling fact: Paul only prayed *three* times for his thorn in the flesh to be removed. Why didn't he ask a fourth and fifth time?

J.I. Packer writes that prayer includes the distinct activity of "accepting from God one's own situation as he has shaped it."[7] I believe that is what Paul did. He accepted his situation as being from the Lord. Paul knew that God is *able* to take the thorn away. And certainly, God is *willing* for his children to be healthy and well; that's within the scope of his holiness and love. Yet, God didn't heal Paul. Instead, he said, "My grace is sufficient for you." Apparently, that was all Paul needed to hear to cause him to stop asking.

Perhaps Paul was more interested in God getting the credit and glory. I think Paul saw the bigger picture. He realized God would get more glory by his thorn *not* being removed. The Lord didn't have to say "no" to Paul. It wasn't a matter of God being unable or unwilling to do it. Of course he was. God simply showed Paul a better way to glorify his Savior through his life.

For Paul, it came down to a matter of wills—his will versus God's will. In Day 1 of this week, we talked about the importance of praying first for God's will to be done on earth, before we begin asking for things for ourselves (i.e., going through the HE part of the prayer model before we pray the WE part). If we want his will above our will—if we truly want his kingdom to come—then we should opt for that which brings the Lord the most glory through our lives.

Look again at the prayer need you wrote down at the beginning of this lesson. Run the following checklist on that request to help you identify whether it meets the guidelines we've studied in this lesson. Be sure to prayerfully check all you feel are true at this time.

_____ I believe God is able to accomplish my request.

_____ I believe God is willing to grant this kind of request.

_____ I am asking God over and over to answer this request.

_____ Above all I want God's kingdom to come and his will to be done.

Praying the Prayer

I want to show you some arm gestures to help you remember the prayer model better. First, hold your arms up toward the sky as you quote the HE section of the Lord's Prayer. Next, wrap your arms around yourself as you quote the WE section. For the last section, THEY, slowly stretch your arms out in front of you (signifying opening them to others). Please do this exercise several times this week as you pray through the Model Prayer. Practice now as you pray and journal the three sections of prayer.

HE – Vertical

Remember to try not to refer to your needs and personal concerns as you journal this first stage of prayer, which is your time to honor and adore the King and surrender yourself to him. Keep it vertical focused on the Lord.

WE – Personal

Write down something that concerns you right now. It could be a financial problem or an issue at work or at home. Share your needs as a prayer to God.

THEY – Kingdom

Pray for someone besides you and your family. It might be your neighbor or someone you go to school or work with. Pray for other people's needs instead of your own now.

There is one more qualification we need to consider in order for our prayers to be heard and answered. We must pray from pure hearts. "You do not have, because you do not ask. And when you do ask, you do not receive, because you ask with wrong motives, that you may squander it on your pleasures" (James 4:2-3 BSB). Before you ask for anything, pray first for God to reveal to you your true motives for asking. Pray like David: "Search me, O God, and know my heart! Try me and know my thoughts! And see if there be any grievous way in me, and lead me in the way everlasting!"

JOURNAL

DAY 3: *FORGIVE US*

For several years I traveled as a music evangelist. I was privileged to lead thousands in musical praise. One of the songs most often requested was called *He Paid a Debt*. The lyrics include these words: "He paid a debt he did not owe. I owed a debt I could not pay. I needed someone to wash my sins away." The older I get and the longer I walk with Christ, the more I realize how true those words are and how much I desperately need God's forgiveness.

Today our focus is on an essential request in the Model Prayer: "Forgive us our debts, as we also have forgiven our debtors" (NIV). I feel sorely inadequate to try to unearth the rich, relatable depths of this passage. Who among us is able to comprehend all the truths nestled in these words? So, let's go ahead and wave the white flag. Let's stop and ask the Author of this prayer to grant us much-needed insight and enlightenment. You pray first; then I'll pray:

"Most holy God, your name is set apart from all others. Your ways are high above the heavens, and your thoughts are far beyond our thoughts. Your written Word can only be understood and applied as we are taught by the Holy Spirit. Please open our eyes today to see what you want us to realize and respond to from this lesson. We trust you and love you, and we thank you in advance. In the name of Jesus, Amen."

Foreshadowing Prayer

When Jesus said to pray "Forgive us our debts," he was in essence prophesying his own death. He knew there was no way our sins could be forgiven without his blood being shed on the cross. When we come to this part of the Model Prayer we should pause briefly and remember why we have the privilege to pray those powerful words. We can pray "Father, forgive us" because of Jesus' awesome and horrific sacrifice at Calvary.

Oswald Chambers expressed it well: "Forgiveness is the divine miracle of grace; it cost God the Cross of Jesus Christ before He could forgive sin and remain a holy God…When once you realize all that it cost God to forgive you, you will be held as in a vice, constrained by the love of God."[8]

Family Prayer

We have the privilege to pray the Model Prayer because of our salvation. This prayer is not a prayer *for* salvation. That's an important distinction. Prayer for salvation is explained in Romans 10:9, 10, and 13. The Lord's Prayer, on the other hand, is based on a *relationship* that already exists between us and God. It can only be prayed by those of us who know God as "our Father."

The reason we pray for our sins to be forgiven in the Model Prayer is not so we can go to heaven. Instead, we should make a habit of seeking God's forgiveness in order to maintain our *fellowship* with the Lord. God is a holy God who will not commune with us when we have sin in our lives. It's like a household in which harmony and camaraderie are broken between parents and children when the child disobeys and does something that he or she knows the parent disproves of.

Read 1 John 1:5-10. According to this passage what can prevent us from having fellowship with God? In verse 9, what is the remedy John gives to repair our broken fellowship with the Lord?

An evangelist friend of mine shares a powerful illustration. He says sin is like pebbles thrown into a stream. At first, they seem harmless. But as more and more pebbles are thrown, they build up and become a dam, which stops the flow of water. He said that is how it is with our sins. We must ask the Lord to get down in the stream bed, so to speak, to clean it out and clear away our sins. Only our Savior can do that. Then the joy, peace, and power of the Holy Spirit can flow in our lives once again.

Be careful not to lump all your sins together when you confess them. We should be specific in naming our sins. And while we should be quick to confess known sins, we should not make up things that are not true. We are to pray, "Forgive us our sins," not what *might* be sins. The Greek word for "confess" in 1 John 1:9 means to *speak the same thing* and to agree with and admit.[9] How can we "say the same thing" as God says about our sins and agree with it if he hasn't convicted us of them yet?

Forsaking Prayer

Notice Jesus prayed, "Forgive us of our *debts.*" You may have learned it as "trespasses" or "sins," but the Greek word Jesus used literally means "that which is owed, a debt."[10] "Forgive us for what we owe" is what Jesus said we should pray. That is a deeper thing than a trespass. Trespassing is the breaking of a law. One might trespass into a place he or she shouldn't be, for example. We can admit in court our guilt for trespassing and possibly receive forgiveness for it. Judges can pardon us for breaking the law.

Remember though, the Model Prayer is based on God not as our judge, but as our heavenly Father. Judges don't have an investment in us. Judges simply serve to pass judgment. We owe them nothing. There is no connection between us and a judge beyond that moment in the courtroom. There is no long-term relationship. Thus, we are not *indebted* to a judge.

A father, on the other hand, has a great investment in his child. In a real sense children "owe" their fathers a debt of gratitude and service for what has been deposited into their lives. Because we trusted Christ, God is our Father. He invested in us with the blood his Son Jesus shed on the cross. In 1 Corinthians 6 Paul says, "You do not belong to yourself, for God bought you with a high price" (vs. 19b-20a).

When we do something we should not do or fail to do something we should, when we harbor an attitude or grudge we should not harbor, we are in essence *holding back* a little part of us from the Lord. It's like we are saying, "No God, you can't have this part of me." Problem is, God already owns that part of us. We are taking from God what is rightfully his. He bought us. Thus, by us taking back what belongs to the Lord, it becomes a "debt" we owe to God.

How do we pay such huge debts to the Lord? We can't. There is absolutely nothing we can do or say that will reclaim the time we wasted or negate the sin we committed against a holy God. All we can do is come empty-handed to him, fall on his grace, and say, "Father, I am sorry. Humbly I ask you to forgive me of my debts for not giving to you my all."

As we read in 1 John 1:9, we are forgiven when we confess our sins. The slate of our heart is wiped clean. The offense is gone and forgotten by God (praise the Lord!). However, it is not enough to just confess; we must also *forsake* our sins. Here's why: If all we ever do is confess, then we are treating God merely as a judge. We have no obligation to him beyond that moment. He pardons us, and we go away forgiven until we sin again. Then we come back to God, ask his forgiveness, and he grants it. We go away until we sin and need him again. We act as though there is no relationship and no obligation between the confessions.

I don't want to just have him wipe the slate clean when I mess up, do you? I want to give him the marker that made the bad marks to start with.

I don't want to go back and do something stupid again. I want to *forsake* that sin and turn it over to him. That is because he is my precious Father whom I love because he first loved me. He has invested his Son's life in me. Jesus paid it *all*. All to him I owe. I don't want to rob God by taking any part of me back again. I want to say, "Lord, here is the marker of my life. Please draw a beautiful picture with it, as only you can do. I fall at your feet and trust your grace. I am completely yours. Do with me what you want."

℣ If that is your heart's cry, then stop and review the prayer you just read. Pray it as your own. Stay here in this place for a few moments. Let your heart catch up with your mind. Confess any "debts" you owe to God, and trust him to forgive you here and now and restore you.

Forgiving Prayer

Our understanding of forgiveness is not complete—we cannot get the full picture—without the remainder of this request. "Forgive us our debts, *as we also have forgiven our debtors*" (NIV, italics mine). It is as though Jesus said all of that in one breath. I think sometimes we see those as two different ideas, when in fact they are one continuous, congruent thought.

I believe Jesus naturally assumed we would forgive others. That is because the two have to happen together. You cannot really have one part of that sentence without the other. That would be absurd. If we have sincerely been forgiven, then we should want others to be forgiven also. Notice Jesus did not say "as long as we forgive others," or "because we forgive others." It is not a contingency plan or a comparison. We don't forgive to be rewarded. Love and good will for others should flow supernaturally from our forgiven hearts.

℣ Read Matthew 18:21-35 now. Based on this parable why do you suppose God is so serious about us forgiving other people? How many times did Jesus say we should be willing to forgive others? Think about what he said. Does that seem a bit unreasonable to you, for God to expect so much of us?

Keep in mind that the Model Prayer is more than mere words we utter occasionally. It should be our lifestyle. And if we have truly walked through the first part of the prayer model, then we should want to forgive others. Paul urged Christians to "be kind to each other, tenderhearted, forgiving one another, just as God through Christ has forgiven you" (Ephesians 4:32). That is God's *will*, and we are praying for his will to be done on earth.

In the Sermon on the Mount Jesus said, "So if you are presenting a sacrifice at the altar in the Temple and you suddenly remember that someone has something against you, leave your sacrifice there at the altar. Go and be reconciled to that person. Then come and offer your sacrifice to God" (Matthew 5:23-24). One of the reasons *we* need to go to those who have offended us is that *our* hearts may be more humble and right before the Lord than theirs at that moment. Thus, we may be more receptive to God's leading to go and reconcile.

But let's face it: Forgiving those who have harmed us can be very difficult. In his amazing book, *The Peacemaker*, Ken Sande writes, "Forgiveness can be extremely costly, but if you believe in Jesus, you have more than enough to make these payments. By going to the cross, he has already paid off the ultimate debt for sin and established an account of abundant grace in your name. As you draw on that grace through faith day by day, you will find that you have all that you need to make the payments of forgiveness for those who have wronged you."[11]

This morning I read a heart-wrenching post on Facebook. I don't know this lady or her husband personally, but what she wrote wrecked me nonetheless. I want to share a portion of her entry with you.

"Today I am mad...We've started a new chapter. Scratch that—a new book. Our lives will be completely different in the days, months and years ahead. They will be different because a man set out to 'run over a cop' and that 'cop' was my husband. That 'cop' was Conner and Chloe's dad. That 'cop' was a man that put his heart in to his community he represented when he put on his badge, the groups he represented when he volunteered, a 'cop' that put his heart into his family. That 'cop,' his life has forever been changed because a man set out to 'run over a cop.' Right now I cannot see myself forgiving that man who sent a text stating 'I am going to run over a cop I think.' He did what he said he was going to do. He ran over my 'cop.'"

I have to say I honestly do not know how I could forgive that man. I certainly cannot judge this broken and grieving wife for her hesitancy to forgive. But this I do know: I can do all things through Christ who gives me strength (Philippians 4:13). Every day we should be breathing in and breathing out forgiveness. Breathe in our own forgiveness because of Jesus' work on the cross for us and breathe out forgiveness for others because of the Holy Spirit who loves and forgives through us.

Praying the Prayer

You may have noticed the word "us" throughout the WE section of the prayer model. This portion should include burdens and concerns you have for your family and friends and for people you care deeply for. Take time to list those people and situations now. You might want to write them in your prayer journal where you can refer back to them in the weeks and months to come. Lay them each before the Lord in prayer today, and trust him with each situation concerning "us."

JOURNAL

Living the Prayer

Vance Havner writes, "We are not capable of judging our own selves and our work for we are too close to it and likely to color the verdict in our own favor. Even if our conscience is devoid of offense and our heart does not condemn us, we may not make a correct appraisal. Things may not be right in the sight of God when they are satisfactory to us. We are too prejudiced in our own behalf to give an unbiased estimate."[12] Who might you be prejudiced against? Who might you need to forgive or ask for forgiveness? Ask God to reveal to you what you may be harboring deep inside and what you may need to do to be reconciled today.

JOURNAL

DAY 4: *LEAD US NOT*

"Lead us not into temptation" is perhaps the most confusing request in the Model Prayer. It sits at the pinnacle of the Model Prayer, and yet, it is hard to understand and make sense of.

Theologically, it just doesn't really work. Regardless of how one translates the word "temptation," it doesn't seem to hold theological water, so to speak. How can it mean "temptation to sin" when according to James 1:13, God tempts no one? If it means trials and testings, Jesus said it is a fact that we will have tribulations (John 16:33). James also addresses that topic, saying, "When your faith is tested, your endurance has a chance to grow. So let it grow, for when your endurance is fully developed, you will be perfect and complete, needing nothing" (1:4b-5).

Considering, then, that God doesn't tempt us and that trials can be good and even necessary, why should we ask him not to lead us into temptation? What an odd thing to pray, wouldn't you say?

It is important to remember the Lord's Prayer is more than something we recite on Sundays at church. Jesus meant it to be a lifestyle prayer—something we can pray in every season of our lives, during both the highs of life and the lows.

Perhaps the greater purpose of this request is to cause us to have to dive deeper than a mere intellectual understanding of what we pray. As he moves us through this model for prayer, it is as though the Lord is slowly peeling away our layers to get to the very core of who we are. Of the three requests within the WE section of the prayer model—for provisions, purification and protection—it is this third request that can best reveal our utter vulnerability and humanity. As one commentator explains it, "The words are a cry issuing from a deep sense of our personal weakness against the powers of evil."[13]

Admit

As finite beings our understanding is often limited and short-sighted. "Lead us not into temptation" is a challenging request because it is difficult to understand. It's hard to wrap our minds around why we should pray those words or what they mean. They seem to contradict what we've been taught about temptation. Honestly it's hard to make good sense of them in our heads.

Yet, isn't that how it is in *life* sometimes too? Are there not days when we feel like we are lost in a fog and things don't make sense to us? We don't know what to think or how to comprehend our situation. Life can come down on us so hard at times that we're not even sure what we believe anymore.

For some time, I have been mentoring a man in his mid-twenties. He's walked with the Lord since he was a young child. He has always maintained a strong witness for Christ, and he continues to be faithful to his church and his calling. Over the past few years, however, he has been through some dark valleys. People and things he loved and counted on have been ripped away from him. He has been through more heartache and turmoil in his short life than many Christians twice his age. As a result, he struggles with depression.

While we were talking the other day, he intimated to me what he was feeling. He said, "I know God loves me, but I don't think he likes me." Now, that is obviously a bogus statement. God both loves and likes his children. And on days when my young friend is thinking more clearly, he would tell you that. In fact, he knew when he said those words they were not true. But he wasn't speaking from his head to me that day; he was spilling from his heart—a very human and broken heart.

That reminds me of another man who spoke from a broken heart. It was the God-man, Jesus Christ, in the Garden of Gethsemane. As he prayed to his Father, he too said things that might not make sense to someone who has never experienced brokenness.

Read now the heart-rending account in Matthew 26:36-45 of Jesus' grueling experience praying in the Garden. What words did Jesus utter that might seem unusual or unexplainable? What about his prayer seemed to contradict what he taught and why he came to earth?

Jesus told his disciples that "everything written about me in the law of Moses and the prophets and in the Psalms must be fulfilled" (Luke 24:44). Several of those prophecies were about his death on a cross. Jesus must have realized it was not possible for that cup to pass from him. Yet he prayed, "If it is possible..." Why would he do that? Why pray such seemingly useless words?

I believe Jesus was experiencing a very *human* moment. He wasn't trying to use logic and reason. He was being honest and open about what he felt. His prayers were spilling from the depths of his crushed soul. As one theologian describes it, our Lord was revealing the natural and

86

necessary limits of his humanity.[14]

When we consider the horror of what was ahead for Jesus, we can start to identify with his desperate plea to escape that suffering. The human part of us does not feel his prayer to be strange or unusual. After all, wouldn't we do the same if we were in his place?

The reality is that deep inside we are but weak mortals. We cannot handle the struggles of life on our own. We need divine intervention. Could it be that by asking God not to carry us into temptation we are in reality recognizing our limited understanding? Could it be that God wants us to *admit our human frailty* and our desperation for him?

Fortunately for us, it is our *Father* we are praying to; thus, what we say to him does not have to be filtered or make logical sense all the time. Thankfully, "he is tender and compassionate to those who fear him. For he knows how weak we are; he remembers we are only dust" (Psalm 103:13-14). Hallelujah!

Acknowledge

When we ask God not to bring us into temptation, admitting our frailty is not the only thing we are doing. We also *acknowledge his sovereignty.* Think about it: When you are faced with something as scary as a temptation, who you gonna call? To reference an old movie, you're not going to call ghostbusters. They can't handle this for you. You need to call on someone who is powerful enough to truly help you.

So, who is that going to be? At the risk of sounding absurd, you can't call up Satan and say, "Hey, could you hold off your demons for a day or so? I need a break from temptation for a while." No, you and I can only go to one source for help with temptation. And that is to the One who lords over all things, including Satan himself. 1 John 4:4 assures us that "he who is in you is greater than he who is in the world" (ESV). Our God is greater! The cosmic powers over this present darkness can do nothing unless God gives them permission.

♪ Read Job 1:6-12, and then read Job 2:1-7. Who was in charge in those heavenly scenes? Who was calling the shots? What had to happen before Job could be bothered and attacked by the devil?

At the Last Supper Jesus said to Peter, "Simon, Simon, Satan has asked to sift each of you like wheat. But I have pleaded in prayer for you, Simon, that your faith should not fail" (Luke 22:31). From this one verse we can discern some powerful lessons about temptation. First, we discover that even Jesus while on earth relied on prayer to help overcome the enemy. Also, because Satan had to ask God for permission to sift Peter, we see once again that El Elyon is sovereign and in charge. As with Job, Satan had to go through God first.

So it is with us as his children. Nothing can happen to us unless the Lord approves of it. That does not mean we will not be tempted. Peter was tempted; Jesus was tempted, and we will be tempted too. Nonetheless, we can rest assured in these powerful truths: God is our heavenly Father who loves us dearly, and he wants to use us for his glory on this earth. He will help us overcome each temptation we face. Our God is able! I love how Warren Wiersbe explains it: "As believers, we have this confidence: God is always in complete control. When God permits Satan to light the furnace, he always keeps his own hand on the thermostat!"[15]

Align

Thus far we have seen that to pray "Lead us not into temptation" is to admit our frailty and to acknowledge God's sovereignty. But is that all we mean when we make that request? Is that enough? I don't think so. Here's why...

The demons aren't really bothered by us admitting we are needy humans. They probably laugh at us for finally coming to realize what they have known about us all along. "Getting honest" before God and expressing our true feelings can be good for the soul, but alone it accomplishes very little.

Does it make demons nervous when we acknowledge that God is in charge? Perhaps. But anybody can call him "Lord." Jesus said, "Not everyone who calls out to me, 'Lord! Lord!' will enter the kingdom of Heaven. Only those who actually do the will of my Father in heaven will enter" (Matthew 7:21). So, as important as it may be, acknowledging God for who he is still is not quite enough to rattle the forces of darkness. What *does* get their attention is believers who have the *will* to back up the words they pray.

In *Screwtape Letters*, C.S. Lewis' fictitious novel about temptation, the devil's high assistant, Screwtape, explained the importance of a person's will to his demon nephew, Wormwood. In one of his letters to Wormwood, he wrote: "Think of your man [that you are tempting] as a series of concentric circles, his will being the innermost, his intellect coming next, and finally his fantasy...you must keep on shoving all the virtues outward till they are located in the circle of fantasy." Screwtape went on to explain, "It is only in so far as they reach the Will and are there embodied in habits that the virtues are really fatal to us [as demons]."[16]

In other words, virtues only matter when they affect our will. Good intentions don't defeat the enemy—right actions do. That is why it is vital we do more than admit our frailty and acknowledge his sovereignty; we must also *align to God's authority* and will. Each day, we must "put feet to our prayers" and demonstrate that we mean what we are praying.

We have already seen how Jesus' words in the Garden of Gethsemane revealed his humanity. He did not try to hide his struggles. He told his disciples, "'My soul is crushed with grief to the point of death. Stay here and keep watch with me.' He went on a little farther and bowed with his face to the ground, praying, 'My Father! If it is possible, let this cup of suffering be taken away from me'" (Matthew 26:38 39).

I am glad Jesus let us glimpse his "human side" there in the Garden. I am thankful he can relate to us because of his humanity. But I am even more grateful and indebted that he did not use his humanity as an excuse. He did not allow his feelings to rule him.

In that pivotal moment, as the fate of souls hung in the balance, our precious Lord abandoned his own will and completely submitted to his Father's will. Matthew Henry writes, "He prayed that, if possible, the cup might pass from him. But he also showed his perfect readiness to bear the load of his sufferings; he was willing to submit to all for our redemption and salvation."[17] Oh, what a Savior!

Attitude

Think of a temptation or trial you are faced with from time to time. What is your attitude toward it? If it is a temptation to sin, do you succumb to it sometimes? Are you secretly okay with that? Or do you try to resist it? Do you *really* want to overcome that temptation? If it is a trial of some sort, are you feeling defeated by it? Is it making you bitter toward God or other people? Have you been tempted to throw up your hands, curse God, and quit? Be honest with yourself right now.

No matter how fervently we pray for help avoiding temptation and overcoming evil, if we have a nonchalant or passive attitude toward any of it, then we will most likely fail. If there is even a small part of us that enjoys and desires opportunities to sin, then we are setting ourselves up for sure defeat.

"Lead us not into temptation" should be far more than familiar words we chant from time to time. They should represent the attitude of our heart to not fail our Lord—to not give in to temptations and to always trust him through the difficult times of life. We must do more than pray to avoid temptation and trials; we must choose everyday to die to ourselves and live for God alone.

Praying the Prayer

Think again about a temptation or trial you are facing. Bring it before God now.

- Admit you are unable to handle it on your own.
- Acknowledge you need his power and wisdom.
- Align yourself now with what he wants you to do and with his authority over you.

Write a prayer of confession and surrender to the Lord for any wrong attitudes about it.

JOURNAL

Living the Prayer

In our next lesson we will look at strategies to overcome evil and temptations. However, no strategy can be effective until we have first made up our mind to follow Jesus and please him no matter what the cost. Several times today and this week recite Jesus' words in the Garden, "Not my will but yours be done." Declare them over and over to yourself and as a prayer to God. Say those words alongside "Lead us not into temptation." Pray them both like you really mean them.

JOURNAL

DAY 5: *DELIVER US*

Jesus placed the subject of evil in a prominent place in the Lord's Prayer. "Deliver us from evil" is at the pinnacle of the Model Prayer, along with the exhortation to "lead us not into temptation." The reason was not, mind you, to bring honor to evil. That would be absurd to think. However, he apparently wanted his followers to appreciate the gravity of this necessary topic. Evil is not to be taken lightly, and as we will prayerfully see today, it is not to be ignored. It is to be treated with the greatest care and attention.

ℰ My hope is that today's reflection on evil will ultimately lead us to adoration of our awesome God. Take time to praise him now. Tell him how awesome and hallowed he is. Also, ask the Lord to deliver you from any thoughts at this moment that might try to distract you from this important lesson. The devil would love nothing more than to keep you and me from uncovering his wicked schemes and evil ways.

The two requests for protection in the WE section of the Model Prayer are tightly connected and should be prayed together. "Lead us not into temptation" answers the question of *what* we should be concerned about. "But deliver us from evil" answers the question of *why*: Why should we pray not to be led into temptation? Simply put, it is because temptation can lead to evil. That is why these two requests are inseparable.

If we pray these requests everyday as a habit, what can they help us accomplish spiritually? Great question! I'm sure there are many benefits, but I want us to focus on three in particular today:

1. The Model Prayer calls our attention to evil.

I grew up in a small town in the countryside of Alabama. There was very little crime in that area back then. We felt so safe, in fact, that we didn't even lock our doors at night. My friend Scott Dawson, on the other hand, lived his early years in the inner city of Birmingham, so he learned to watch his back and stay alert to possible danger. Scott and I traveled together for several years in full-time evangelism. One night in Pensacola, Florida, we were sitting in a restaurant after a church service. I will never forget him telling me he thought the guys sitting near us were watching us and "scoping us out," as he put it. I told him he was paranoid, and I naively kept eating my food.

When we finished our meal and got up to leave, those guys got up from their table as well. When we paused near the register after paying, they also waited. That was enough to convince Scott he might be right about their evil intentions. On the way out the door, there was a man selling his paintings. So Scott thought fast and struck up a conversation with the man. Sure enough, the suspicious characters didn't walk past us. They continued to wait behind us. Scott asked the man with the paintings if he had more in his vehicle. The man said he did, so we proceeded to walk out to the man's car. The ill-intentioned guys followed us out and waited in their van until we got in our vehicle to leave. As we drove out of the parking lot they followed us onto the street. They continued to follow us to a nearby police station where our scary stalkers finally drove on past and left us in peace.

Unfortunately, evil is all around us, even if we don't realize it. As Paul wrote, "For our struggle is not against flesh and blood, but against the rulers, against the authorities, against the powers of this world's darkness, and against the spiritual forces of evil in the heavenly realms" (Ephesians 6:12).

One of my earliest "wake-up" calls to the idea of demonic activity came when I read a novel titled *This Present Darkness*. It is the story of a pastor who finds himself engaged with powers of darkness in spiritual warfare over his small town and church. Here is an excerpt from the first chapter where two angelic beings are fighting a demon just outside the pastor's church:

> "There was an explosion of suffocating vapor, one final scream, and the flailing of withering arms and legs. Then there was nothing at all except the ebbing stench of sulfur...The big blond (angel) replaced a shining sword as the white light that surrounded him faded away.
>
> "A spirit of harassment?" he asked.
>
> "Or doubt...or fear. Who knows? And that was one of the smaller ones."
>
> "But what are they doing here? We've never seen such a concentration before, not here."
>
> "Oh, the reason won't be hidden for long." He looked through the foyer doors and toward the sanctuary. "Let's go see this man of God."[18]

Of course, this dialog is from a fictitious novel. We have little idea how demons and angels actually operate on earth. Nonetheless, Scripture seems clear that they are real and that spiritual conflict, unseen to our human eyes, takes place more often than we care to imagine.

♪ Read 2 Corinthians 10:3-5. What do you believe Paul meant by "war" and "strongholds" and "weapons"? Have you given much thought to the idea of spiritual warfare? According to this passage, what part should we as Christ-followers play in this unseen conflict?

2. The Model Prayer prompts us to ask for deliverance from evil.

Thoughts of evil lurking around us and spiritual warfare might unnerve and even scare some. But remember Jesus' words to his disciples: "I have said these things to you, that in me you may have peace. In the world you will have tribulation. But take heart; I have overcome the world" (John 16:33 ESV). Our God has overcome death, hell, and the grave! He won, and we can win too. We should not be frightened or intimidated by evil; instead, we should pray each and every day for the Lord to deliver us by his mighty hand. God is constantly holding back the tide of evil that would discourage, distract and destroy us. Praise his name that he is all-powerful and able to overcome evil for good in our lives!

Still, one might wonder why we should have to *ask* for deliverance. Why does God allow people to experience evil in the first place? Or, put in a more familiar way, why do bad things happen to good people? Those are important questions. It is not within the scope of this study to try to answer them fully. But consider this: If we think we are "good" we are terribly misguided and mistaken. Jesus said, "No one is good except God alone" (Mark 10:18 ESV). When we begin to grasp our utter depravity as humans and how deserving we are of death, the question stops being, "Why do bad things happen to *good* people?" Instead, we are compelled to ask, "Why don't *more* bad things happen to *bad* people like us?"

Clearly, praying the Lord's Prayer does not insulate us from all harm. There are plenty of examples of godly saints who died martyrs' deaths. Why didn't God deliver them? That's another excellent question! Think about Stephen and Paul. They both died for their faith; yet, evil did not overtake them. Their deaths were allowed by God in his perfect timing. Many were saved as a result of their persecutions. And think about Jesus: He willingly laid down his life on the cross. He gave his life freely. No person or demon took it from him. Through his death he brought redemption for mankind. God won the ultimate battle for our souls. He overcame evil with his awesome goodness.

You see, God wins every time, and as we follow and submit to him and trust in him, we win also. According to Revelation 20, Satan will one day be cast into the lake of fire, and we will reign with Christ forever. What a mighty God we serve!

3. The Model Prayer leads us to avoid evil when possible.

If we are sincere in asking God to deliver us from evil, if we understand how devastating it can be to yield to temptation, then we will want to avoid evil at all cost. The Lord's Prayer isn't a "Get-out-of-evil-free card." We can't merely pray this prayer and then mindlessly walk through our day with our guard down. We have an important role to play. We must *choose* to "fear the Lord and turn away from evil" (Proverbs 3:7b).

In order to win a war, soldiers need to know the tactics of their enemy and the strategy to defeat them. Fortunately, the Bible gives us clear instructions on how to overcome temptation and evil.

Read Ephesians 2:1-3. Look closely at verses 2 and 3. Try to identify three distinct sources of temptation. They are listed below in this lesson, but try not to peek. See if you can spot them on your own.

People often give Satan sole credit for every temptation they experience. While he is the ultimate instigator behind all sin and blasphemy toward God, the devil himself is often not the source of our temptations. As we read in Ephesians 2, there are actually three sources of temptation. They are the world (the value system of this age), the flesh (our old nature that is prone to sin), and the devil (aka, Satan, or perhaps one of his demons).

Years ago, I heard Dr. Adrian Rogers share a simple but profound outline to help us remember how to win in each arena or source of temptation. I encourage you to commit the outline below to memory, as well as the Scripture verses listed with each.

World > Faith

There is much to enjoy and envy in this world, and as Christians it might seem like we are missing out on certain pleasures that our non-believing friends often indulge in. As David said, we mustn't worry about the wicked or "envy those who do wrong. For like grass, they soon fade away...The lowly will possess the land and will live in peace and prosperity" (Psalm 37:1, 2, 10 NLT).

We can't touch and feel the treasures we are storing up in heaven or

94

see the amazing home Jesus is preparing for us. We have to accept those things by *faith*. 1 John 5:4b declares, "This is the victory that has overcome the world—even our faith" (NIV). There is an old hymn which powerfully sums up this idea:

Turn your eyes upon Jesus
Look full in his wonderful face
And the things of earth will grow strangely dim
In the light of his glory and grace.[19]

Flesh > Flee

God created us with certain human desires. In and of themselves they are not bad. We enjoy eating food, for example, and (thankfully) that is a good thing. But if we eat too much food too often, then we are being gluttonous, and that is not good. God made sex to be enjoyed within the confines of marriage. But sex outside of marriage is evil and sinful.

No matter how much faith we might have, it will not be enough to overcome the desires of our human nature in heated moments of temptation. 2 Timothy 2:22 says, "Flee the evil desires of youth and pursue righteousness, faith, love and peace, along with those who call on the Lord out of a pure heart." That is exactly what Joseph did when he was tempted by Potiphar's wife. Genesis 39:12 says he tore himself away and ran from her so fast that "he left his cloak in her hand"! We must be wise like Joseph and *flee* temptations of our flesh.

Devil > Fight

Sometimes, no matter how much faith we have and regardless of how willing we are to flee, temptations still manage to find us. I have been in worship services singing the Lord's praises and exhibiting lots of faith in him, when suddenly, an unholy thought has raced across my mind. I wasn't hanging out in some seedy, tempting situation. I wasn't giving "place to the devil," as Ephesians 4:27 warns. I was in church, for crying out loud!

In such unlikely moments and places, it may be Satan or one of his demons who is directly tempting us to sin. They want to draw us away by our own lust, and they will lie and do everything in their dark power to convince us to give in. Those are the times we must "put up our dukes" and *fight*.

James 4:7 says, "Submit yourselves therefore to God. Resist the devil, and he will flee from you." The next time you believe you are being tempted by the devil, resist him. Say, "In the name of Jesus, get behind me, Satan." Also be sure to quote Scripture, as Jesus did when he was tempted in the wilderness in Luke 4.

Keep in mind that Satan cannot read your thoughts. Therefore, say the words aloud. If you were resisting arrest, you wouldn't only say something inside your mind, would you? You would speak out loud to those opposing you. You would even repeat your words to them if needed, wouldn't you? In the same way, be adamant to resist the devil. He must flee if you truly resist him. Just be sure to resist in the powerful name of Jesus and not in your own (pitiful) strength and name.

Praying the Prayer

Take time now to pray for your family and friends. Intercede for them to resist falling into temptation and to be delivered from the evil around them. Thank your Savior for showing mercy to you and your family and for not giving you what you really deserve. Allow yourself time to get lost in wonder, love and praise of your awesome God.

Living the Prayer

James 4:7 gives an important prerequisite to overcoming the devil. It says we must first *submit* ourselves to God. Satan can sense if you are not sincere. You will be powerless to defeat him if your heart is not completely yielded to God first. Do a heart exam on yourself right now. Better yet, be still before the Lord and ask *him* to reveal any ill motives or hidden sins. Now, walk through your day aware and on guard against evil and sin. Be sure to pray for and journal about your family and friends.

JOURNAL

WEEK 3 FOLLOW-UP QUESTIONS FOR GROUP DISCUSSION

1. What does it mean to say that Christians are to be salt and light in this world?
2. If you had been Paul and Silas in prison at Philippi, do you think you would've stayed where you were in order to be salt and light when the doors opened and the chains fell off? Why do you think they had the courage to remain?
3. What are some ways Christians today can bring heaven to earth?
4. Is it easy or hard for you to ask God for the things you need? Why do you think that is?
5. How hard is it for you to "[accept] from God [your] own situation as he has shaped it," as J.I. Packer wrote about prayer? Why do you think people sometimes struggle to find something to ask forgiveness for when they pray?
6. What does this statement by Oswald Chambers mean: "It cost God the Cross of Jesus Christ before He could forgive sin and remain a holy God"?
7. Why would we pray daily for our sins to be forgiven when they have already been forgiven on the day we accepted Jesus as our savior?
8. Why is it important to remember that, when we pray the Model Prayer, asking God's forgiveness for our sins, we go to him as our heavenly Father and not as our judge?
9. Why do you think God's children might ever feel, as did the young man I was mentoring, that God loves them but doesn't like them?
10. How important is it to align our will with God's authority and will? Why does doing that help us?
11. How do you think faith helps us be victorious over temptations the world lures us into?
12. What does it "look like" to "flee the evil desires of youth and pursue righteousness, faith, love and peace…" (2 Timothy 2:22)?
13. Are you comfortable saying (aloud!) "In the name of Jesus, get behind me Satan"? Why or why not?

Footnotes for Week 3:

[1] Dwayne Moore, *Pure Praise: A Heart-focused Bible Study on Worship* (Colorado Springs, Colorado: Group Publishing, 2008), 26.

[2] N.T. Wright, *"On Earth as in Heaven,"* N.T. Wright Online, May 20, 2007, https://ntwrightpage.com/2016/03/30/on-earth-as-in-heaven/

[3] *ibid.*

[4] Voice of the Martyrs, *Hearts of Fire: Eight Women in the Underground Church and Their Stories of Costly Faith*, (Bartlesville, Oklahoma: VOM Books, 2015), 178-179.

[5] Anadara Arnold/Carl Cartee/Elias Dummer, *Honestly,* All For The King Music/AUTOTUNES/Lakeside Media Group/Postage Stamp Publishing/Willow Branch Publishing, 2012.

[6] R.A. Torrey, *How to Pray* (Chicago: Moody Publishers, 2007), 17.

[7] J.I. Packer, *Praying the Lord's Prayer* (Wheaton, Illinois: Crossway, 2007), 17.

[8] Oswald Chambers, *My Utmost for His Highest* (New York: Dodd, Mead and Company, 1935), Dec. 8.

[9] Strong's Concordance, "3670 homologeó," *Bible Hub,* https://biblehub.com/greek/3670.htm.

[10] Strong's Concordance, "3783 opheiléma," *Bible Hub,* https://biblehub.com/greek/3783.htm.

[11] Ken Sande, *The Peacemaker* (Grand Rapids, Michigan: Baker Books, 2004), 208.

[12] Vance Havner, *The Vance Havner Devotional Treasury*, (Grand Rapids, Michigan: Baker Books, 1976), 124.

[13] Pulpit Commentary, "Matthew 6:13," *Bible Hub,* https://biblehub.com/matthew/6-13.htm

[14] Elliot's Commentary for English Readers, "Luke 24:44," *Bible Hub,* https://biblehub.com/luke/24-44.htm

[15] Warren Wiersbe, *The Strategy of Satan* (Carol Stream, Illinois: Tyndale House, 1979), 35

[16] C.S. Lewis, *The Screwtape Letters* (New York: Harper Collins, 1996), Letter 6

[17] Matthew Henry's Concise Commentary, "Matthew 26:39," *Bible Hub,* https://biblehub.com/commentaries/matthew/26-39.htm

[18] Frank Peretti, *This Present Darkness* (Westchester, IL: Crossway Books, 1986), 12.

[19] Helen Howarth Lemmel, *Turn Your Eyes Upon Jesus*, Warner Chappell Music, Inc, 1922.

WEEK 4 KINGDOM PRAYER

For thine is the kingdom, and the power, and the glory, for ever. Amen.
Matthew 6:13b KJV

DAY 1 *FOR*

Welcome to our fourth week of study! What a journey we have been on already, and I'm trusting it will continue to get even better as we dive deeper into more incredible truths within the Model Prayer.

I want us to begin today with an extended time of prayer. For this experience to be most impactful and effective, we first need to *prepare* to pray. Here are some important steps to help:

- If possible, get in a quiet place where you are alone to pray. Do not lie down when you pray. Consider sitting in a straight-backed chair at a table, so you can write and concentrate better.
- Turn over your phone so you can't see if anyone messages you. Turn down the ringer and the alerts.
- If you are using a computer or tablet for this lesson, try to close any social media apps you may have open so you can't tell if/when you receive likes and comments.

Okay, let's begin now. I will give you some suggestions as we go along, but this is your time, so you pray as you feel led.

HE *(Praise & Surrender)*

Begin by reciting the first part of the Model Prayer: *"Our Father who art in heaven, hallowed be Your name. Your kingdom come; Your will be done, on earth as it is in heaven."*

🎵 Read aloud Psalm 95:1-7a. Read it with boldness and conviction.

🎵 Now read all of Psalm 145. Don't lose focus as you read. Think about every word as you say it. Read it twice, if needed, to really grasp it.

🎵 Pray directly to God, praising and calling him by some of his names. (Refer to the list of God's names at the end of Week 2: Day 4 to refresh your memory.)

🎵 Consider singing a song of praise to the Lord, something that tells of God's goodness and greatness, like *How Great Thou Art, How Great Is Our God, Goodness of God,* or another worship chorus or hymn you know by heart.

🎵 Pray a prayer of praise to God now. Keep it vertical, focusing on him and not yourself. Perhaps include some of the names of God you used or words of the song you sang or ideas you got from today's Scriptures.

🎵 Meditate on the following passages. Read them slowly and thoughtfully.

> "Then Jesus said to his disciples, "If any of you wants to be my follower, you must give up your own way, take up your cross, and follow me. If you try to hang on to your life, you will lose it. But if you give up your life for my sake, you will save it. And what do you benefit if you gain the whole world but lose your own soul? Is anything worth more than your soul?" (Matthew 16:24-26 NLT).

> "And so, dear brothers and sisters, I plead with you to give your bodies to God because of all he has done for you. Let them be a living and holy sacrifice–the kind he will find acceptable. This is truly the way to worship him. Don't copy the behavior and customs of this world, but let God transform you into a new person by changing the way you think. Then you will learn to know God's will for you, which is good and pleasing and perfect" (Romans 12:1-2 NLT).

🎵 Now, breathe a prayer of thanksgiving and surrender to the Lord. Pour out your heart to God in complete submission to him and to his will over your own. Commune with him as friend with friend (because he *is* your Friend!).

Stay in the HE section of the prayer until your mind is set "on things that are above, not on things that are on earth" (Colossians 3:2). Go back through this section again if that is what it takes to focus your mind and heart completely on the Lord.

WE

Take time now to pray for yourself and your loved ones. Be specific with your requests and pray for your loved ones by name.

Provisions: *Give us this day our daily bread.*
"And this same God who takes care of me will supply all your needs from his glorious riches, which have been given to us in Christ Jesus" (Philippians 4:19).

Purification: *Forgive us our debts as we forgive our debtors.*
"Hide Your face from my sins and blot out all my iniquities. Create in me a clean heart, O God, and renew a right spirit within me" (Psalm 51:9-10).

Protection: *Lead us not into temptation but deliver us from evil.*
"Stay alert! Watch out for your great enemy, the devil. He prowls around like a roaring lion, looking for someone to devour" (1 Peter 5:8).

So, now that you have prayed, how do you feel? Have you been reminded you are forgiven and free? Are you more focused? I hope so!

Here's another question: Are you *finished*? Or, do you somehow feel there is more you should pray about, as though you have left out something significant? Perhaps you feel there was something missing from this prayer experience. Well, in fact, there may have been.

I want you to think deeper than merely reciting words of the prayer. Think more substantively than that. Consider the *content* of your prayer. Where did you concentrate most of your focus just now? It was on the Lord and on yourself and on those you care for, correct? What or whom did you *not* mention or think about during your prayer time? I think it's safe to assume the answer is anything or anyone outside your sphere of personal concern.

And that is precisely why the third part of the Model Prayer is so vital. We need spiritual eyes to see beyond our own little world to the great big world Jesus came to save.

THEY

Please say that last part now: *"For Yours is the kingdom and the power and the glory forever. Amen."*

As you may guess, this final section is more comprehensive in its application. With the simple conjunction *for,* we suddenly transition into an expansive formula or doxology that can broaden our thinking and open our minds and hearts. We refer to it as the THEY section because it can lift our sights beyond just our own circles of personal and family concern. It should lead us to pray for people we wouldn't normally think of or whom we're not closely related to or in contact with. But why is that? It is because of the implication of these powerful words: *"For yours is the kingdom."*

When Jesus came to earth, he came preaching, "Repent of your sins and turn to God, for the kingdom of Heaven is near" (Matthew 4:17). When he sent out his disciples, he told them, "Go and announce to them that the kingdom of Heaven is near" (Matthew 10:7). The focus was on the *kingdom.*

The kingdom, among other things, includes a realm of people. God is all about people. God so loved this world that he sent his only begotten Son to die on a cross. We, too, should care for those that he loves and died for. We should "pray to the Lord who is in charge of the harvest…to send more workers into his fields" (Luke 10:2). We need to pray for the harvest to be plentiful. Why? Because the greater the harvest, the more souls are added to the kingdom.

Please note it is not our responsibility to "build" God's kingdom. That is his job. However, we should be concerned for the kingdom and seek to advance it. We should want people to be added to God's kingdom. We are called to be salt and light to the world. Therefore, we should be faithful to proclaim the message of hope, so more and more people can come to saving faith in Christ. We need to pray beyond just WE and also pray for THEY who make up his kingdom around the world. Furthermore, we should be burdened for the countless millions who don't know Christ and aren't part of his awesome, eternal kingdom of light.

Burdens

Unfortunately, many of us don't have the time or capacity to be burdened for other people because we are too laden with our own worries and problems. It reminds me of the popular nursery rhyme, *There Was an Old Woman Who Lived in a Shoe*. This lady was the epitome of being burdened down:

> There was an old woman who lived in a shoe.
> She had so many children, she didn't know what to do.
> She gave them some broth without any bread;
> Then whipped them all soundly and put them to bed.

Sounds like that lady needed to learn to pray the Model Prayer and cast her cares on the Lord. I think this version of the nursery rhyme has a much better ending

> There was an old woman
> Who lived in a shoe,
> She had so many children,
> And loved them all, too.
> She said, "Thank you Lord Jesus,
> For sending them bread."
> Then kissed them all gladly
> and sent them to bed.[1]

This "old woman" had the right idea! She knew where her help came from. She wasn't fretting; instead, she was praising and thanking Jesus. She was ready to bear other people's burdens because she had cast her own cares on the Lord. That's the way we should all learn to live! Our God is faithful and can handle all our problems if we'll just lay them at his feet.

Jesus' Example

Interestingly, the last part of the Lord's Prayer (aka doxology) is not in the most reliable manuscripts. While it was included in the oldest Alexandrian or Egyptian text, it was later omitted "on overwhelming authority" by Greek scholars of the Lord's Prayer. That shouldn't really discourage us, however, from still including it when we pray. As one commentator explained it, the church's inclusion in "using the doxology is fully justified by its contents; for it places us more emphatically than ever in a right relation to God."[2] I like what J.I. Packer said about it: The doxology of the Lord's Prayer "is not in the best manuscripts. Nevertheless, it is in the best tradition!"[3]

Jesus included the kingdom in the opening section when he said, "Thy kingdom come." Thus, we know for certain that the word *kingdom* was part of his model of prayer. Whether he actually prayed "Yours is the kingdom..." at the end of the prayer, we can't know for sure. What we do know is that Jesus *lived out* what those words represent. He lived an expansive life that placed other people's needs ahead of his own. He healed the sick, raised the dead, showed compassion for outcasts, and encouraged the downtrodden. He cared relentlessly for people, most of whom were outside his circle of family and friends.

In his Sermon on the Mount, Jesus said, "God blesses you who are poor, for the kingdom of God is yours" (Luke 6:20). As he spoke those words, he was probably gazing on a vast group of listeners mostly made up of people who were *literally* poor. He loved the "nots" of the world– those who were not popular, not noticed, not top of their class, and not significant or important in society. I'm glad he still cares for the "nots," for I am one of them! Thank God he cares for *all* of us.

As Jesus walked through the final days of his time on earth, he modeled the pattern of the famous Prayer he had taught to his disciples. One might say he "gave feet to his prayer." In the Garden of Gethsemane Jesus prayed for himself. It was there and then that he took care of the HE and WE portions of the Prayer. He surrendered to his Father's will. The Lord got up and walked out of that garden knowing he had laid his tremendous burden before his Father. Now he was ready to bear the burdens, the *sins*, of the whole world. Within a few hours, he would face his greatest test: having to fully embrace the final part of the Model Prayer. All he was about to do and go through he would do for other people and for his Father's kingdom and glory.

On a hill called Calvary, Jesus the Christ allowed soldiers to violently nail him to a cross. As he hung there between heaven and earth, he looked down upon the very ones who had just driven spikes through his wrists and feet, and he prayed for them. With his hands outstretched, he said, "Father, forgive them for *they* don't know what *they* are doing." They were the ones he interceded for, for they were the ones he loved, even as he writhed in unimaginable pain.

Isaiah 53 says, "Surely he took up our pain and bore our suffering, yet we considered him punished by God, stricken by him, and afflicted. But he was pierced for our transgressions, he was crushed for our iniquities; the punishment that brought us peace was on him, and by his wounds we are healed. We all, like sheep, have gone astray, each of us has turned to our own way; and the Lord has laid on him the iniquity of us all" (v. 4-6).

Jesus carried the iniquities of all mankind–including your sins and mine. When he prayed "Father, forgive them," he was also praying for *us*. His arms were stretched open wide for the whole world. If the Son of God could care that much for us and be that unselfish, if he was that determined to intercede for us, shouldn't we likewise take time to pray for others? *They* need our prayers, because *they* need our Lord.

Living the Prayer

Clearly God is burdened for others to know his Son. Ask him to transfer some of that deep burden and love to you. Ask him to help you think more expansively and lovingly toward people–even those who are very different from you and whom you might even consider your enemies. Write out names of those you are praying for today.

JOURNAL

Praying the Prayer

Stretch out your arms now and pray for people who come to your mind. Try to call them by name as you intercede for them. Walk through your day looking for ways to "Bless those who curse you, and pray for those who spitefully use you" (Luke 6:28 NKJ).

JOURNAL

DAY 2: *YOURS*

According to Pastor Tim Keller, books on prayer "tend to be primarily theological or devotional or practical, but seldom do they combine [those] all under one cover. A book on the essentials of prayer should treat all three."[4] In visioneering this study, my aim was to write comprehensive lessons that feature those very things. While I've tried to consistently include all of them each day, sometimes one area receives more attention than the others. Such may be the case today.

We have come to the topic of the kingdom of God. Because of the sheer volume of content on this subject, we need to cover a great deal of information. I will do my best not to make it feel like a history lesson or academic exercise. But if it does, so be it, for in order for us to be accurate and effective in our prayer lives, we need a foundational and functional understanding of solid doctrine.

𝄢 To help get your mind more engaged with this important topic, let's start with a question: When you think of the kingdom of God, what comes to your mind? Take a moment to soak on that.

The Lord's Prayer is deeply rooted in and saturated with the subject of God's kingdom. I fear many Christians are like I was for so long, praying for the kingdom to come to earth, and yet having little understanding of what his kingdom actually is. Thus, as students of the Model Prayer, we are compelled to learn more about the kingdom. So, let's jump head first into the deep end! Take a big breath; we could be under a while!

Some Prehistory

In order to get a better grasp of the kingdom of God, we need to go all the way back to before the dawn of creation. The sphere where God ruled his kingdom was the heavens, and his subjects were the created angelic beings, whose purpose was to administrate God's kingdom and worship him. For example, we know from Isaiah's vision in Isaiah 6 that the seraphim surrounded and overshadowed the throne of God day and night, crying "Holy, holy, holy, is the Lord Almighty" (v. 3). So, we see that God instituted a kingdom in the realm of the heavenlies that was made up of angelic beings. Because all were subject to the Lord who ruled as king, there was perfect harmony within the kingdom.

But then, somewhere during the expanse of timeless millennia, things took a turn for the worse when one of the angels went rogue and started stirring up trouble in the kingdom. Ezekiel describes a king that many scholars believe represented an angelic being who fell from his prominent place in heaven. That angel was Lucifer, otherwise known as Satan.

Read Ezekiel 28:1-19 now. Highlight any words or phrases that give you clues about Lucifer's status while in heaven and the circumstances that led to his downfall.

Lucifer had been the wisest and most beautiful of God's angelic beings. He had the privilege to minister in the presence of God before his throne. But he became filled with pride. He sinned by rebelling against the very One who had created him. He led a revolt that, based on Revelation 12:4, may have drawn as much as a third of the created angelic hosts to follow after him.

New Sphere

Satan's goal was to be like God and be worshiped and adored as he was. Of course God could have "nipped it in the bud" in heaven immediately after Lucifer became full of pride. He could have wiped out Satan and his followers right then and there. That would certainly have settled the question of who has the right to rule in his kingdom. But instead, God seems to have chosen another method by which to answer the question of who reigns and rules: He created the heavens and the earth.

Dr. Dwight Pentecost was the Distinguished Professor of Bible Exposition Emeritus at Dallas Theological Seminary for many years. He wrote a fascinating book on the kingdom of God, representing years of scholarly research and teaching. In fact, much of what I'm sharing in this lesson was influenced by his teachings. Regarding the heavens and the earth, Dr. Pentecost writes, "This creation was designed to provide a new sphere in which God's kingdom might be administered and through which the question of right-to-rule would ultimately be concluded."[5]

Colossians 1:16b says that God "made the things we can see and the things we can't see—such as thrones, kingdoms, rulers, and authorities in the unseen world. Everything was created through him and for him." It's important to take note of the last two words in that verse. All things were created *for him.* Thus, we can conclude, at least in part, that the earth was brought into existence to manifest God's sovereign will where he could work out his divine purposes.[6]

Kingdom Came

Over just five days God created the heavens and the earth, the waters, the sun and moon, the birds and the animals. Then, on the sixth day, the Lord produced his most prized creation. He created human beings, two of them to be precise. He breathed into them his very own breath and made them into his likeness. They had a mind to know God, a heart to love him, and a will to obey him. They got to commune face to face with their Creator. Apparently, he would sometimes walk with them "in the cool of the day" (Genesis 3:8). They were his people, and he was their God.

In effect, God prepared in the Garden of Eden a kingdom on earth over which he would rule. And he placed Adam there to oversee it. Dr. Pentecost wrote, "God delegated authority to man to rule as His representative."[7] He saw that what he had created was "good." Thus, on the seventh day, the Lord rested.

With the establishment of the magnificent and peaceful Garden of Eden, God's kingdom on earth was a paradise. Satan and his hordes were nowhere to be seen, and life was good in the Garden for Adam and Eve. They could literally have lived happily ever after. But things didn't work out that way. Often in classic fiction stories, just when things seem to be resolved, another crisis happens and things get bad again, and that is certainly true in this far-from-fiction account in Genesis.

Man did not fare well in the miniature theocracy God had put him in charge of, and it didn't take him long to royally mess things up. Satan showed up eventually, and when he did, he was cleverly disguised as a serpent. He came to Eve and tempted her there in the Garden. That infamous scene and pivotal moment marked the beginning of the end for Adam and Eve–and the devil too, for that matter.

Read Genesis 3:1-7 now. How exactly did the serpent tempt Eve? What convinced Eve to give in and eat the fruit?

1 John 2:16 lists three sources from which temptations can come. They are 1) the lust of the flesh, 2) the lust of the eyes, and 3) the pride of life. Eve experienced all three sources of temptation. Verse 6 says, "She saw that the tree was beautiful [lust of the eyes], and its fruit looked delicious [lust of the flesh], and she wanted the wisdom it would give her [pride of life]. Thus, she took some of the fruit and ate it."

Eve and Adam disobeyed God and ate the fruit he had told them not to eat. It wasn't that the fruit was poisonous or bad, for everything God created was good. Rather, God used that particular tree to test their willingness to submit to his authority. They were not to assume that just because they had been put in charge of God's kingdom in the Garden they were somehow independent of his laws and rule. Those in the kingdom must obey the rule of the King (and so it still is today).

Two Kingdoms

So, how are you doing? Need to come up for some air? We will soon! I told you this could be a little heavy on the doctrine side. Try to hang in there a few more minutes. There are some really important truths we still need to discover...

When Satan revolted against God, he proceeded to set up his own version of a kingdom. Initially, the devil's kingdom had only existed in the heavenly realm where only angels were subject to his authority. But now that Adam and Eve had sinned and experienced spiritual death, Satan's kingdom was established on earth, and they became his first human subjects.

From that point forward everyone born in Adam's line would be born into the kingdom of darkness. According to Romans 5:12, every human being has a nature of sin that was passed down from Adam. Because of this sin, two kingdoms developed side by side in the earthly realm.

All through the Old Testament, one can see how both kingdoms were in operation on the earth. The influence of Satan's kingdom as well as God's kingdom continued to unfold. When Jesus came on the scene in the New Testament, the first message he preached was "Repent of your sins and turn to God, for the kingdom of Heaven is near" (Matthew 4:17). John the Baptist proclaimed that same message. The kingdom of God got lots of "press" and attention by the writers of the New Testament. All told there are more than 140 references to God's kingdom within the Gospels and the Epistles.

On the other hand, there are very few references to the devil's kingdom in the New Testament. Jesus only referred directly to Satan's kingdom once. In Luke 11:18 when he said, "If Satan is divided against himself, how can his kingdom stand?" his reference was in passing, to make a point to the Pharisees regarding how kingdoms can't be divided among themselves. Paul made a brief reference to the devil's kingdom in his letter to the church at Colossae. He writes, "For [God] has rescued us from the dominion of darkness and brought us into the kingdom of the Son he loves" (Colossians 1:13). But Paul only mentions Satan's kingdom in order to bring contrast and emphasis to the awesome kingdom the Church is now part of in Christ.

Interestingly, neither Jesus nor Paul put any real weight or attention on Satan's kingdom. No New Testament writer did. Why do you suppose that is?

And consider the Lord's Prayer: While there is a reference to delivering us from evil in the prayer, there is no clear acknowledgment of the devil's kingdom. It would seem, in fact, that the reference to evil in one sentence gets immediately upstaged and downsized by the focus on God's kingdom in the next sentence: "...deliver us from evil because yours is the kingdom..."

Let's zero in now on the words, "Yours is the kingdom." Think about what could be implied when we say that. It could be taken to mean there is only one kingdom. For hundreds of years, that familiar doxology has been recited by millions. Yet to our knowledge, no one has ever really questioned the exclusivity of that statement. Since there are in fact two kingdoms, why not at least *mention* the other kingdom? Wouldn't it be more accurate to pray, "Yours is *one of* the kingdoms?" Why say, "Yours is *the* kingdom?"

Here is my take on why the kingdom of God is emphasized in Scripture and in the Model Prayer: I believe it's because his is the only kingdom that will really matter in the end. It is the Lord's kingdom that will last forever. Therefore, it is his kingdom we should focus on and build our future hopes and dreams around.

No Worries

What do you say we head to the surface now and grab some air? I think we've had enough "kingdom diving" for one day. But as we're getting out and drying off, there is one more thing that I think will encourage you...

Clearly Satan's kingdom exists. Both Jesus and Paul acknowledged it, and the Lord's saints have battled the kingdom of darkness for centuries. We shouldn't ignore it. We should pray against evil and be on guard against the devil and his demons.

Nonetheless, we should never be intimidated or worried about the enemy's kingdom. You know why? It's a *false* kingdom; that's why. And

Satan's reign is a false reign. He is not the one who is ultimately in charge. God is. "He who is in you is greater than he who is in the world" (1 John 4:4b ESV).

As you walk through your day, keep this powerful truth always before you: Our God reigns. Pray often and with fervency: "The true and lasting kingdom belongs to you, O LORD!"

Praying the Prayer

Take time to pray and journal through each section of the Model Prayer now.

HE – Vertical
When we praise God, we are essentially seating him in a place of authority in our lives, affirming that we know that his is the kingdom. Along with the seraphim who surround his throne day and night, we can worship him as we cry, "Holy, holy, holy is the Lord God Almighty!" Sing or say the words of this powerful song of praise:

Holy, holy, holy! Lord God Almighty!
Early in the morning our song shall rise to thee;
Holy, holy, holy! merciful and mighty,
God in three persons, blessed Trinity!

Holy, holy, holy! All the saints adore thee,
Casting down their golden crowns around the glassy sea;
Cherubim and seraphim falling down before thee,
Who wert and art and evermore shalt be.

Holy, holy, holy! Though the darkness hide thee,
Though the eye made blind by sin thy glory may not see,
Only thou art holy; there is none beside thee,
Perfect in power, in love, and purity.

Holy, holy, holy! Lord God Almighty!
All thy works shall praise thy name, in earth and sky and sea;
Holy, holy, holy! merciful and mighty,
God in three persons, blessed Trinity![8]

WE – Personal

Write in your journal about concerns that may be obscuring God's kingdom for you right now. If you have loved ones who seem to know or care little about his kingdom, pray for their salvation.

JOURNAL

THEY – Kingdom

Pray that others outside your personal sphere will seek God's kingdom, acknowledging him as Lord of their lives.

JOURNAL

Living the Prayer

Commune with the Lord from your heart as you build this vital pattern of prayer into your daily routine. Pray through the parts of the Model Prayer at least two times today.

DAY 3: *KINGDOM*

In my quiet time this morning a verse in Isaiah jumped out at me, and I want to share it with you: "For since the world began, no ear has heard and no eye has seen a God like you, who works for those who wait for him!" (64:4).

♪ Before we get into the lesson today, we need to start by being in awe of our awesome God. Meditate on that verse in Isaiah for a few minutes. Wait before the Lord, and then pray a prayer in response to his greatness and goodness in your life.

Today's lesson will be more interactive than some. Please be sure to take good notes and engage in each question and activity. These are important to help you synthesize the information we'll be talking about.

The goal for today is two-fold: to understand how God's kingdom relates to the Lord's Prayer and to understand how the Lord's Prayer relates to the kingdom. What we discover today should leave us more encouraged and determined to build the pattern of the Model Prayer into our daily lives.

What Qualifies as a Kingdom?

The Greek word for kingdom in the New Testament is *basileia*, which means royalty, rule, or a realm.[9] In Bible times, in order for a kingdom to qualify as a kingdom, it needed three things: the right to rule, a realm to rule, and the reality of rule. People who lived back then understood what a kingdom was. In our modern age, however, we aren't as familiar with theocracies and monarchies. Thus, we need to take a close look at what the three qualifications mean and why they matter.

First of all, in order to qualify as a kingdom, a kingdom needs a king. It needs someone who has the *right to rule*, someone who has received *authority* to rule over the kingdom. We know, of course, that God has the solemn right to rule over his creation. Psalm 103:19 declares, "The LORD has established his throne in the heavens, and his kingdom rules over all." And according to Hebrews 12:2, Jesus "is seated at the right hand of the throne of God."

The second requirement of a kingdom is that it must have a *realm of rule*. A kingdom's realm is made up of subjects, of people. It is not necessarily a kingdom of land or objects. Jesus said, "The kingdom of God is near! Repent of your sins and believe the Good News!" (Mark 1:15). Because only *people* can repent, the kingdom must include a realm in which kingdom authority is exerted over people.[10]

The Jews are God's chosen people, but thankfully, though, because of Jesus' sacrifice, we Gentile folks have been grafted into the vine (Romans 11:17). We too are a "chosen people, royal priests, a holy nation, God's very own possession" (1 Peter 2:9). John 1:12 says, "But to all who believed him and accepted him, he gave the right to become children of God." Imagine that. If we know Christ, we get to be royal subjects in God's forever kingdom. Oh, what grace the Father has lavished on us!

The third necessary ingredient of a kingdom is the *reality of rule*. This refers to the active exercise of royal authority. A king can *say* he has a kingdom, but if he's not actively ruling over people, then he doesn't really possess a kingdom. Conversely, those who aren't under the king's rule are *not* part of his kingdom.

We can rest assured our God is on the Throne actively ruling today. All through Scripture and throughout history there is clear evidence of God's sovereign hand and activity. Daniel 4:17 states, "...the Most High is sovereign over all kingdoms on earth and gives them to anyone he wishes and sets over them the lowliest of people." Leading Abraham from Ur, directing Noah to build an ark, saving the Israelites from slavery in Egypt, sending Jesus to die for our sins—all of these are examples of God actively working and moving in the world.

How Can the Kingdom Affect Our Prayers?

I want us to blend the qualifications for God's kingdom with the sections in the Model Prayer. The following table shows how they correlate with each other. Please take time to thoughtfully answer the questions that are below the table.

HE	Right to Rule
WE	Realm of rule
THEY	Reality of rule

How should knowing God has the right to rule affect the way you pray the HE section? How should his kingly authority affect your acts

114

of praise and surrender?

    🗝 How should the realm of God's rule affect the WE part of your prayer? What difference should it make knowing you are a valued subject in his kingdom?

    🗝 How should the reality of God's rule affect the THEY part of your prayer? What should it motivate you to do when you think of the people who are not part of his kingdom and not living under the Lord's blessings and rule?

What's Unique about the Kingdom?

There are many wonderful things about the kingdom of God that make it fascinating and unique. Unfortunately, we don't have the time needed to do an extensive study on the kingdom. Instead, we will focus on three vital characteristics of God's kingdom, which I think can help us better grasp its connection to how the Model Prayer relates to the kingdom.

I'm hoping to "build a case" for the first characteristic so you can guess it on your own. To help see and understand it, we need to look at three passages in the New Testament.

Clue #1: Luke 17:20-21 says, "One day the Pharisees asked Jesus, 'When will the Kingdom of God come?' Jesus replied, 'The Kingdom of God can't be detected by visible signs. You won't be able to say, 'Here it is!' or 'It's over there!' For the Kingdom of God is already among you'" (NLT). The Pharisees were looking for an outward show, but Jesus said it can't be "detected" by outward signs. If the kingdom isn't visible and outward, then that must mean it is invisible and *internal.*

Clue #2: When Jesus stood before Pilate he said, "My Kingdom is not an earthly kingdom…my Kingdom is not of this world" (John 18:36). Jesus' kingdom couldn't be seen by Pilate because it was "not of this world." That could mean it was a spiritual, *internal* kingdom.

Clue #3 is found in Romans 14. The church at Rome was arguing about which day of the week they should observe as the Lord's Day and whether they should eat meats offered to pagan gods. It had apparently brought such confusion and division within the church that Paul was prompted to write some stern words to them about it.

    🗝 Read what Paul told them in Romans 14:14-19. Pay particular attention to verse 17. That is where we will find our third clue.

Here is a summary of Clue #3 based on verse 17: Meat and drink are things we take in from the outside of ourselves. The kingdom of God, however, is not about outward things. It is about righteousness, peace and joy in the Holy Spirit. Those things are on the inside of us. They are *internal.*

Internal

Based on all the clues we have gathered, can you guess what aspect of the kingdom we are thinking of? It is this: The kingdom of God is based on *internal relationship.* Or to be more exact, the kingdom of God on the earth at this time is located in the heart of every believer.

In the passage we just read in Luke 17, Jesus told the Pharisees, "the kingdom of God is already among you." Wherever Jesus went on earth he brought the kingdom of God with him. That's because Jesus is the reigning King of kings and Lord of lords. John Piper writes that the statement "'Jesus is Lord' is almost synonymous…with the kingdom." It is declaring "the king has come."[11]

Now the kingdom of God has moved inside of us as his followers because he lives in us. That is what Paul meant in Romans 14 when he said, "righteousness, peace and joy *in the Holy Spirit*" (italics mine). God gave us a new heart—a spiritual heart transplant—when he put his Spirit inside of us. That's what places us into his kingdom. That's what makes us his royal subjects. It's the power of the Gospel that brings about this phenomenal change. I think some of us have forgotten how powerful the gospel is to radically transform someone's life.

Just the other day I got a message from Loretta. She wrote to thank me for leading her to Christ years ago. Although it has been a long time, I still remember it vividly. We were around a bonfire during a youth event at our church where we shared the plan of salvation. Loretta, only 15 years old at the time, said, "I want to know Jesus." I remember how she was so overcome with emotion she couldn't even speak. All she could do was whisper, "Thank you, Jesus." I admit I wondered for a moment if she had really prayed to receive Christ. But then, she looked up at me, and it erased all my doubt. The difference in her face was like night to day—or death to life, to be more precise. That is because her heart had been changed. And all these years later, she hasn't gotten over what Jesus did for her. That is the power of the Gospel. That's the transformation God can make in a person's life, internally and eternally!

The *internal relationship* aspect of the kingdom corresponds best with the HE section of the Model Prayer. Because God's kingdom is an internal relationship with him, we can affect the kingdom by *surrendering* ourselves to God and making sure our hearts are focused on him.

Universal

The second unique characteristic of God's kingdom needs no clues to discover. It should be quite obvious. His is a *universal reign*. Because God is omnipotent, the Bible is clear about the unlimited scope of his sovereignty over his kingdom. 1 Chronicles 29:11-12 declares, "Yours, O LORD, is the greatness, the power, the glory, the victory, and the majesty. Everything in the heavens and on earth is yours, O LORD, and this is your kingdom. We adore you as the one who is over all things. Wealth and honor come from you alone, for you rule over everything. Power and might are in your hand, and at your discretion people are made great and given strength."

God is in charge of everything. He is not limited to just his subjects or to a certain realm of rule. As John Piper explains, "He sits as king on his throne of the universe, and his kingly rule—his kingdom and his reign—governs *all things*."[12] God controls the elements; he controls the weather. James 5 says Elijah prayed to the Lord and stopped the rain. God can control people that are not even in the kingdom. He can change the heart of a king, like he did Pharaoh's in Exodus 10-11. That's because God's reign is universal. He is Lord of all, and He can intervene in the affairs of man. Psalm 135:6 says, "The LORD does whatever pleases him throughout all heaven and earth, and on the seas and in their depths."

The universal reign of God correlates best with the WE section of the Model Prayer. Because God's kingdom is a universal reign, we can affect the kingdom by petitioning the Lord of all to intervene in the world and act on our behalf.

External

The third aspect is also vitally important in how it relates to our prayer life. The kingdom brings *external results*. It begins in, then flows from, the hearts of his servants. If we have the Spirit of God inside us–if we are following Jesus, and he's living his life through us—then we bring the kingdom with us wherever we go. There will be external results from that. Even if people don't have his kingdom in their own hearts—even if they don't acknowledge Jesus as Lord--we can still bring his kingdom to them, so that his kingdom is among them and near them.

As Stephen was on trial before the Sanhedrin, "none of them could stand against the wisdom and the Spirit with which he spoke" (Acts 6:10). God was flowing powerfully through Stephen. Those religious rulers could not deny that something was different about him. They may not have known what it was, but God's kingdom was being brought into that room through Stephen.

Incredible things, miracles, in fact, can happen because we are part of the kingdom and shining our light for him. When we ask, we can receive. What a powerful truth: our God intervenes when we pray! James writes, "The effective, fervent prayer of a righteous man avails much" (5:16b NKJV). Knowing he is in charge and wants to answer his children should motivate us to pray for others and lift them up.

External results match up well with the THEY section of the prayer model. Because God's kingdom brings external results, we can affect the kingdom by praying for Christians to be salt and light to the world and by interceding for people outside the kingdom to see Christ in us and be saved.

How Can Prayer Affect the Kingdom?

The relationship between the three aspects we looked at today can be summed up like this: Our *internal relationship* with God and the *universal reign* of God produce *external results* for God.

As we did with the qualifications, let's bring the unique aspects of God's kingdom together now with the sections in the Model Prayer. The following table shows how they all correlate with each other. Look the aspects over carefully and think through how each relates with the other. Then fill in the blanks that are below the table. The statements are taken directly from our lesson today.

HE	Right to rule	Internal relationship
WE	Realm of rule	Universal reign
THEY	Reality of rule	External results

♘ Because God's kingdom is an internal relationship with him, I can affect the kingdom by _____ myself to God afresh each day as a subject in his kingdom.

♘ Because God's kingdom is a universal reign, I can affect the kingdom by _____ the Lord of all to intervene in the world and act on our behalf.

♘ Because God's kingdom brings external results, I can affect the kingdom by _____ for Christians to be salt and light to the world and by _____ for people outside of the kingdom to see Christ in us and be saved.

Praying the Prayer

As you pray the Model Prayer today, take time to meditate on the qualifications and unique aspects of the kingdom and reflect on the ways you can impact it. Journal your thoughts.

JOURNAL

Living the Prayer

You and I can't make anyone be part of the kingdom, and we can't control the kingdom, but we can control ourselves. Can you say that internally, God is on the throne of your heart right now? If not, pray now and ask him to forgive and cleanse you. As you go through your day, check your heart from time to time, and ask yourself, "Is he ruling *me* at this moment?"

DAY 4: POWER & GLORY

Science teaches that what we experience in the physical world every day can be whittled down to four fundamental forces: gravity, the weak interaction force, electromagnetism, and the strong nuclear force. Many scientists believe these forces govern everything that happens in the universe.[12]

For centuries, researchers have attempted to combine all the fundamental forces of nature and how they interact with each other into one grand unified theory. But trying to unify all the natural forces has stumped even the likes of Albert Einstein over the years.[13] An article at Space.com describes the dilemma like this: "Developing a so-called 'theory of everything'…could explain the entire universe. Physicists, however, have found it pretty difficult [to do]…So far, no one has come up with a good way…"[14]

And I predict they never will.

Here's why: Scientists are hoping to discover a single great force of the universe. But God is ultimately that Force. He governs all that happens in all the universe. And no amount of scientific theorizing or research can ever figure him out. Perhaps that's what Paul meant when he wrote, "Oh, the depth of the riches of the wisdom and knowledge of God! How unsearchable his judgments, and his paths beyond tracing out!" (Romans 11:33).

Today our topics are power and glory. When referring to God, those words can't really be separated. They go hand-in-hand. Nonetheless, we need to consider one word at a time, so that we can understand them both more clearly.

Able

We have already established that God is the overarching Force controlling everything. He is the great and all-powerful Creator. But what if he weren't? (Wow, just thinking those words and seeing them typed out in front of me seems blasphemous.) Let me dare ask us again: What if God weren't all-powerful?

Try to imagine the Model Prayer without being able to say, "For yours is the power." What if you had to say instead, "For mine is the power"? Or what if your only option was to say, "The government is the power"? Or the sun or some other object is the power? What if there were *no one* who has the power? If you couldn't say the power is God's and that he is the ultimate Force in charge, how might that affect your prayers?

Fortunately for us, God *is* able. He has all power. His is the power! If that were not true, then he could not be king and ruler overall. Without his power, we would have no reason to pray. Only our Father in heaven is able to answer our prayers and move mountains on our behalf.

♫ Read Psalm 47 slowly at least two times. As you meditate on it, look for statements which support the idea that he is powerful. What evidence can you find listed in this psalm that points to his greatness and power?

The Greek word used for power in the Lord's Prayer is *dýnamis*. It means miraculous power, might, and strength, as in physical power, force, ability, powerful deeds, and marvelous works.[15] It is the word from which we get our English word *dynamite*.

We all know that dynamite blows things up. It obliterates everything within its reach when it explodes. It cannot control itself. Thankfully, God is much more powerful than dynamite, and he *can* control his power. If he couldn't control it, if his power were raw and unrestrained, then we would and should be fearful of it. But we need not worry, because our God is good!

♫ Go now to Psalm 145. Notice how David focuses on God's greatness and power in the first 6 verses. Then, in verse 7, the theme turns to the Lord's goodness. What does David say in this psalm that demonstrates how God can control his power? What motivates the Lord to restrain his great power? Why, for example, is he slow to get angry with us?

I love J.I. Packer's reflections on *power* in the Lord's Prayer. He writes, "The thought is of omnipotent control…Power is the actual mastery that God's rule shows; not, then, naked arbitrary power, like that of a tornado, or a rogue elephant…but unconquerable beneficence, triumphantly fulfilling purposes of mercy and loving-kindness…It is the power by which God is good to all…and raised Jesus from the dead."[16]

We not only serve a great and mighty God; we serve a good and loving Lord. A poignant moment in the Garden of Gethsemane powerfully illustrates this truth. When the soldiers came to arrest Jesus, Peter pulled out his sword and struck the high priest's slave, slashing off his ear. "Put away your sword," Jesus told him. "Those who use the sword will die by the sword. Don't you realize that I could ask my Father for thousands of angels to protect us, and he would send them instantly? But if I did, how would the Scriptures be fulfilled that describe what must happen now?" (Matthew 26:51-54).

When Jesus said, "what must happen now," he was referring to his own suffering, death, burial and resurrection. He was speaking of all that was still ahead and necessary for him to go through in order for us to be saved. As an old gospel song says, "He could have called ten thousand angels, but he died alone for you and me." What love, what greatness, what true power, resolve, and restraint our Lord and Savior showed for us!

🎵 Stop and voice a prayer of praise, thanking God that he holds all power and authority. Take your time. Consider bowing on your knees as you humbly worship him for his greatness.

Perspectives of Glory

While you were praying and praising, did you happen to mention the word *glory*? It's common in times of praise and upward worship to say things like, "Lord, we give you glory." In fact, the doxology of the Model Prayer includes the words "Yours is the glory." But what does that mean?

Let's look closer at the idea of God's glory. When we say we are giving God glory or "Yours is the glory," we are not talking about something he *receives*, as if we were "handing" him splendor or grandeur or majesty or greatness, as it were. The glory that is his is not ultimately something God *gets*, as though more glory could be added to him. It's not something he needs, and it's not something he does. Glory is who God *is*. It's the sum total of all his attributes, acts and character. All glory already *belongs* to him—*His* is the glory.

This is true, regardless of our opinion of him or our decision to give him glory or not. He already has glory all on his own. Maybe you recall how Jesus got into a long, contentious discourse with some Jews over Abraham in John 8. It's a great example of the reality of God's glory. "The people said, 'You aren't even fifty years old. How can you say you have seen Abraham?' Jesus answered, 'I tell you the truth, before Abraham was even born, I Am!' At that point they picked up stones to throw at him. But Jesus was hidden from them and left the Temple" (John 8:57-59). They obviously didn't agree with him or "give" any glory and worship to him. Nonetheless, they couldn't change the *truth* he'd shared or take anything away from who he is.

The Old Testament refers to glory as the "weight" of God. Exodus 40:34-35 says, "Then the cloud covered the Tabernacle, and the glory of the LORD filled the Tabernacle. Moses could no longer enter the Tabernacle because the cloud had settled down over it, and the glory of the LORD filled the Tabernacle." The word for *glory* here properly means "to have weight, to be heavy."[17] So, when the Bible says the glory of God filled the Tabernacle, it literally means the *heaviness* of his splendor, majesty, and holiness filled that place. (Wow!) Perhaps Paul had this phenomenal display of God's glory in mind when he wrote, "For our present troubles are small and won't last very long. Yet they produce for us a glory that vastly *outweighs* them and will last forever!" (2 Corinthians 4:17 NLT, italics added).

Opinions Count

Exodus 40 goes on to say that "the whole family of Israel could see" God's glory hovering over the Tabernacle (v. 38). This glory was the weight of God, his intrinsic, infinite worth which he had graciously chosen to show the Israelites. Surely they were impressed by it! But regardless of their reaction to his glorious display, it could not add to nor diminish his splendor in the least.

While what we may think about the Lord has little effect on *him*, for *us*, it could mean the difference between life and death, in living this life abundantly or in just existing. It's almost as if there's another "side" to glory, if you will. It's our *opinion* of his glory and our response to it. Although God is always glorious and never-changing, how we perceive him can change and will determine whether or not we bring him glory with our individual lives.

The New Testament seems to support the importance of our perception when it comes to God's glory. In fact, the primary word for glory in the New Testament is a word that, at its core, means "opinion." That's the word used in the doxology of the Lord's Prayer: Yours is the *glory*. The idea here of glory includes a person's opinion or estimation of God that results in honor to the Lord.[18]

♫ Look closely at the graphic below. Read down each side and think about how each statement leads to the next under the categories. Then read side to side or left to right. How do these ideas relate to each other? Are some more important than others? What should acknowledging the scope of his glory ultimately lead us to do?

Who God Is	How We Respond
He has intrinsic glory	We estimate his glory
He manifests his worth	We acknowledge his worth
He deserves honor	We give him honor

Two Sides of Glory

Whenever we pray, "Yours is the power and the glory," we are actually doing two important things. First, we are stating truth about who God is. His really *is* the power and glory; that's an unchanging fact. At the same time, if we mean those words we are praying, then in essence we are also giving our heart-felt opinion of him. We're not just reciting words mindlessly; it's what we *believe* to be true based on the evidence of his glory that God gives us. Our goal should always be for our opinions of God to line up with the *truth* about who he is and what he says.

Fringe Benefits

We should meditate on the Lord's power and glory simply because he is our God and King. However, there are some wonderful by-products of acknowledging these traits. These "extra perks" can put even more fire under us to want to pray and live out the prayer model every day!

When we pray "Yours is the...power and the glory," we:

Enhance our opinion of God. Praying through the parts of the Model Prayer–especially the HE section–adds to the "weight" of God in our minds. Focusing often on God's glory improves our opinion of him, and that, in turn, will help us bring more and more honor to him in our everyday lives. (Meditating on his Word and being plugged into a Bible-believing church and small group are also vital to knowing him better.)

Express our praise to God. The Greek word for power in the doxology of the Lord's Prayer is *doxa*.[19] It's where we get the word *doxology*, which means "discourse of praise." Think of the Model Prayer as a crescendo to an ultimate display of worship. Every day we ought to "put our praise on" and choose to adore God.

Experience the glory of God. As we acknowledge and focus on his glory, he reveals more and more of himself to us. 2 Corinthians 3:18 says, "And we all, with unveiled face, beholding the glory of the Lord, are being transformed into the same image from one degree of glory to another. For this comes from the Lord who is the Spirit." What an incredible truth! The more we gaze on him and his glory, the more we are transformed.

♪ Moses experienced the Lord's glory because he walked with God, talked with God, and longed for God. Read Exodus 33:11-23 now. As you do, search for clues that show how Moses walked, talked and longed for God.

Moses invested years walking and talking with God in faith and in holiness. The more he got to know the Lord, the more he trusted him and longed to know him even better. As Moses drew near to God, God drew near to him. So, it can be with us. May our prayer be as Moses': "Lord, show us your glory!"

Praying the Prayer

Take time to pray and journal through each section of the Model Prayer now.

HE – Vertical
As you spend part of your prayer time praising God today, ask him to reveal his glory to you. Journal about how gazing on his glory transforms you. Perhaps listen to a worship song as part of your vertical prayer and praise time.

JOURNAL

WE – Personal
Lay your burdens at the feet of our powerful, glorious God!

THEY – Kingdom
Intercede for others who have not experienced God's awesome power or witnessed his glory; beseech God to reveal his majesty to a world that is not seeking him; pray for the needs of fellow believers, adding your voice to their supplications.

Living the Prayer

John 1:14 says, "And the Word became flesh and dwelt among us, and we have seen his glory, glory as of the only Son from the Father, full of grace and truth" (ESV). If we know Christ, then we have seen and experienced God's glory–this intrinsic, awesome worth of our great God– and have realized it is heavy and bursting with grace and truth! Take time today to thank the Lord over and over. Ask him to continue to reveal himself to you through his Word and through others. Look for glimpses of God's glory around you–in a sunset or a baby's cry or a bird singing or a storm or a fellow believer's praise.

DAY 5: *FOREVER*

This week's emphasis is on the Model Prayer as a kingdom prayer. The goal of this week has been to stretch our minds and help us see beyond ourselves, to think outside the limits of our own little world to include God's "big kingdom" all around us. There is nothing better to help expand our spiritual thinking than the final word of the Lord's Prayer. The concept of forever is often misunderstood and neglected. Many Christians spend little time thinking deeply about it. Yet grasping the significance of eternity can help inform and ignite our prayer lives.

Ecclesiastes 3:11 says, "He has made everything beautiful in its time. He has also set eternity in the human heart; yet no one can fathom what God has done from beginning to end." God has set a "feeling" of the eternal inside of us. C.S. Lewis explains it like this: "If we find ourselves with a desire that nothing in this world can satisfy, the most probable explanation is that we were made for another world."[20] To some degree all people have a sense of forever that transcends this world.

But what does *forever* mean? In the Bible, the word *ever* basically means unbroken and continuous. In other words, it is perpetual and never-ending. And although we may know what those words mean by definition, it is a struggle to grasp the expanse of what they entail.

A few years ago my family took a trip out West from our home in Louisville, Kentucky, to the Grand Canyon in Arizona and Yellowstone National Park in Montana. It was nearly 5000 miles or 8000 kilometers in distance. No one in our group had ever traveled that length in a single trip. Thus, it was hard for us to appreciate just how far we would be going or how long the journey would take us. So we calculated the drive times through each state and then divided the trip into segments of travel. Thinking of the trip as a series of shorter segments made it easier for us to wrap our minds around the great distance we would cover during this marathon vacation and the time it would take us.

In versions of the Bible which include the Model Prayer's doxology, the Greek is translated basically as "For yours is the kingdom, the power and the glory *forever.*" However, a more accurate rendering would be "For yours is the kingdom, and the power, and the glory *for the ages*" (italics added). The Greek word for *age* here means a space or cycle of time, or a series of ages stretching to infinity.[21] Similar to dividing a long trip into segments, thinking of forever as a "series of ages" might assist our finite minds with the concept of an infinite, timeless eternity.

Infinity and Beyond

No matter how hard we may try to understand, some things simply defy logic. In the classic animated film *Toy Story* Buzz Lightyear has a familiar line he uses throughout the movie: "to infinity and beyond!" Think about that phrase for a moment. How can one go beyond infinity? That doesn't make sense. It's not possible to reach the end of infinity, much less overtake it. From our perspective, what Buzz says seems impossible. But isn't that the point Buzz is unwittingly making? Some things are beyond what we as humans can see and comprehend with our limited perspective.

Let's imagine we are some of the first inhabitants on earth. We see a horizon in the distance, and we think to ourselves, "That bright ball in the sky looks like it's just over the mountain. If I walk toward it, maybe I can get close enough to touch it." As absurd as that sounds, why wouldn't we think that? We don't know any better because our point of view is limited to the ground where we're standing. To get a true perspective, we would need to fly high into space where we could look down and see the sun and the earth in relation to each other. Only then could we understand things more clearly.

One humanist philosopher had this to say about Buzz Lightyear's famous quote: "The meaning of 'To infinity and beyond' is that we all think we are trapped in our human limits, without escape…Buzz is showing us the way to recognize the illusion, change the perspective, finally break free and go…where it was previously unthinkable and unimaginable."[22]

I take issue with that statement on a couple of counts: First, we *are* trapped by our human limits, and we *cannot* escape on our own. When it comes to eternity, the reality is that our finite minds can never truly comprehend it. We simply cannot "fly that high," so to speak. We will never fully grasp eternity as humans because we can never fully grasp the Eternal God. Thus secondly, Buzz can't really show us anything of value. Only the Spirit of God can open the eyes of our hearts and help us see eternity from his perspective.

♫ Paul said, "We have received God's Spirit (not the world's spirit), so we can know the wonderful things God has freely given us… [O]nly those who are spiritual can understand what the Spirit means" (1 Corinthians 2:12, 14b NLT). Stop and pray now that the Holy Spirit will speak to you through the Bible and enlarge your understanding today of the significance of eternity.

Forever HE Is God

When we pray, "For yours is the kingdom and the power and the glory forever," we are acknowledging a fundamental truth: that God's kingdom is *eternal.* In so doing, we are really proclaiming that *God* is eternal, because it is his kingdom.

Dr. Timothy George writes, "God's years, unlike ours, do not come and go. They are succeeded by no yesterday, and they give way to no tomorrow. The God of the Bible is not only the Creator of time but also the Lord of time. Unlike human beings who are creatures of a day, God is the one whose steadfast love endures forever, whose faithfulness is to all generations."[23]

♫ To better understand "God's years" and how he perceives time, please read Psalm 90. Take special note of the verses that refer to time or eternity.

Psalm 90:2 says "from everlasting to everlasting you are God," meaning he is God from the most distant past to the most distant future.[24] In other words, God has no beginning and no end. So how should this profound truth about God's eternality impact our prayers? Does it really matter?

To help answer that, ask yourself this question: What if God weren't eternal? At the risk of sounding ridiculous, what if every day you had to wonder whether God is still on the throne, still in charge, and still alive? The HE section of the Lord's Prayer is focused on praise and surrender. But imagine trying to worship a god who is not eternal. Imagine surrendering to a god who may not always be around.

Think about great world leaders. They spout their ideas and make their laws. Yet, once they die, someone else comes along and changes those ideas and laws. Not so with God. Jesus said, "Heaven and earth will pass away, but my words will never pass away" (Matthew 24:35). God's words will never disappear or become obsolete because God will never disappear or cease to be. He will always and forever be alive and in control to enforce his words.

The angel Gabriel promised Mary, "Of his kingdom there will be no end." We never have to wonder if our God is on the throne. He is! We never have to question whether He still loves us. He does! "Jesus Christ is the same yesterday, today, and forever" (Hebrews 13:8).

What confidence and comfort we should have as we approach the Lord in prayer; he reigns forevermore! That awesome truth should prompt us to praise him and surrender to him from all that is within us!

Martin Luther said, "Such a God have we, such a God do we worship, to such a God do we pray, at Whose command all created things sprang into being. Why, then, should we fear if this God favors us? [Those with] trembling spirits ought to look to this consolation in their temptations and dangers."[25]

Forever WE Are His

Read John 10:27-30. What does this passage teach us about our lives with Christ? How secure are we as his children, and for how long will we be secure?

Once Jesus becomes our Shepherd and we become his sheep, nothing can ever change the relationship. Let that sink in: No one can snatch us from his grip. What an amazing truth! What power and grace our Father has! We are secure in Christ unconditionally and eternally, and that should encourage us and embolden us to pray for ourselves and for other believers.

Because we are his children, we are in his favor. Psalm 30:5a says, "For his anger lasts only a moment, but his favor lasts a lifetime." There will never be a day when you and I have to wonder whether we can come before God. He will always be our Father, and we can always approach him in prayer–first to confess if we have sin in our hearts and then to commune as friend with friend.

Because we are his children, we are in his future. In fact, Revelation 22 tells us that one day we will see his face, and his name will be on our foreheads. There will be no more night. We will not need the light of a lamp or the light of the sun, for the Lord God will give us light. And we will reign with him for ever and ever. (Wow!)

Because we are his children, we are his focus. God's eternal purpose centers on Christ and his church. Jesus said, "I will build my church"

(Matthew 16:18). That is what he is doing. Prayer helps advance the church on the earth. As part of God's church, it is our privilege and responsibility to ask, seek and knock in fervent prayer to the Lord.

Forever THEY Are Likely Lost

It's wise to assume that most people around us are not God's children. Many of those we work with or go to school with or pass in the supermarket do not have a personal relationship with Christ. Jesus said, "Enter through the narrow gate. For wide is the gate and broad is the road that leads to destruction, and many enter through it. But small is the gate and narrow the road that leads to life, and only a few find it" (Matthew 7:13-14).

The stark tragedy is that unless a person places faith in Jesus as personal Savior, he or she will go to hell. In Matthew 25:46, Jesus said, "Then they will go away to eternal punishment, but the righteous to eternal life." In this one verse, Jesus speaks of both the righteous and the unrighteous. Apparently, the eternal life Christians enjoy runs parallel to the punishment that non-believers suffer. In other words, hell lasts as long as heaven.

Knowing a person could spend eternity separated from God in hell should shake us up, maybe even cause us to lose some sleep. Paul was so burdened for his fellow countrymen, in fact, that he said, "I could wish that I myself were cursed and cut off from Christ for the sake of my people…" (Romans 9:3). I don't think we will all be held to that high standard of concern. Nonetheless, we are expected to pray and intercede for others. Samuel told the Israelites, "Far be it from me that I should *sin against the LORD* by failing to pray for you" (1 Samuel 12:23, italics added).

Someone wisely said, "Where there's no burden, there's no bother." As we make a habit in our lives of praying the Model Prayer daily and following its pattern of HE, WE and THEY, it should lead us to a deeper concern for the lost. The more we pray for others, the more willing we'll be to inconvenience ourselves in order to reach them. We'll be more likely to engage with people we don't know (and perhaps we don't really like or understand). Instead of looking for ways to avoid others, we will want to bring as many with us to heaven as we possibly can.

Let's pray the prayer model backwards today.

Begin with THEY. Write out names of people you feel led to pray for now. Allow the Spirit to fill your mind with those he wants you to lift up before him. Pray for others so they may be made whole. Remember that "the prayer of a righteous person is powerful and effective" (James 5:16).

JOURNAL

Now pray for WE. Lay your burdens before the eternal God. Trust him to hear you and answer your prayers because you are his eternal child.

JOURNAL

Close with a time of praise and surrender, for HE is worthy! Read the passages below aloud. Worship your Lord in the splendor of holiness.

"The Lord is King for ever and ever!" (Psalm 10:16).

"The Lord sits enthroned over the flood; the Lord is enthroned as King forever" (Psalm 29:10).

"O God, we give glory to you all day long and constantly praise your name" (Psalm 44:8 NLT).

"For this God is our God for ever and ever; he will be our guide even to the end" (Psalm 48:14).

"I will ever sing in praise of your name and fulfill my vows day after day" (Psalm 61:8).

"Then we your people, the sheep of your pasture, will praise you forever; from generation to generation we will proclaim your praise" (Psalm 79:13).

"I will exalt you, my God the King; I will praise your name for ever and ever. Every day I will praise you and extol your name for ever and ever. Great is the Lord and most worthy of praise; his greatness no one can fathom" (Psalm 145:1-3).

"Then I heard every creature in heaven and on earth and under the earth and on the sea, and all that is in them, saying: 'To him who sits on the throne and to the Lamb be praise and honor and glory and power, for ever and ever!' The four living creatures said, 'Amen,' and the elders fell down and worshiped" (Revelation 5:13-14).

"The kingdom of the world has become the kingdom of our Lord and of his Messiah, and he will reign for ever and ever" (Revelation 11:15).

Living the Prayer

Sing a song of praise before the Lord now. Worship him with your voice and with your heart! Close your time by reciting the Lord's Prayer. Be sure to include a hardy and loud amen at the end to signify you meant all you have prayed. Keep that song and prayer with you as you go through your day.

WEEK 4 FOLLOW-UP QUESTIONS FOR GROUP DISCUSSION

1. Discuss the journal entry you wrote at the beginning of the Day 1.
2. Whom or what did you pray for during the THEY segment at the beginning of Day 1?
3. What song can you think of that best describes Jesus' sacrifice for God's kingdom? If you can't think of one, what would be a good title for a song like that?
4. Do you find it hard to believe that Eve could be so tempted by Satan in the Garden that she disobeyed God? Why or why not?
5. Would you have eaten the fruit, do you think? Explain your answer.
6. How would you explain God's kingdom to someone who's never heard of it before?
7. Which do you think is the strongest source of temptation? Why?
8. Discuss the significance of the following statement in this lesson: "If we have the Spirit of God inside us—if we are following Jesus, and He's living His life through us—then we bring the Kingdom with us wherever we go. There will be external results from that."
9. How can prayer affect the kingdom, according to Day 3: Kingdom?
10. What is one instance of God's great power you have witnessed yourself? OR Describe a time when you have had a glimpse of God's glory.
11. Share a worship song that describes or makes you aware of God's glory. (You don't have to sing it!)
12. This lesson asks you to "imagine trying to worship a god who is not eternal...surrendering to a god who may not always be around." Write an imaginary journal entry for the day on which you have discovered that God is not eternal. Share with group.
13. Pick one or two favorite praise scriptures recorded at the end of the lesson (or another one you like). Explain to the group why these are meaningful to you.

Footnotes for Week 4:

[1] Marjorie Ainsworth Decker, *The Christian Mother Goose Book*, 1978, https://en.wikipedia.org/wiki/There_was_an_Old_Woman_Who_Lived_in_a_Shoe.

[2] Pulpit Commentary, "Matthew 6:13," *Bible Hub* https://biblehub.com/matthew/6-13.htm.

[3] J.I. Packer, *Praying the Lord's Prayer* (Wheaton, Illinois: Crossway, 2007), 106.

[4] Tim Keller, *Prayer: Experiencing Awe and Intimacy with God* (New York: Penguin Random House, 2014), 1.

[5] J. Dwight Pentecost, *Thy Kingdom Come* (Grand Rapids, Michigan: Kregel Publications: 1995), 28.

[6] *ibid.* p. 29.

[7] *ibid.* p. 33.

[8] Reginald Heber, *Holy, Holy, Holy*, 1826.

[9] Jeremy Relm, "The Four Fundamental Forces of Nature," *Space.com*, October 01, 2019, https://www.space.com/four-fundamental-forces.html.

[10] Elizabeth Howell, «Unified Field Theory: Tying It All Together,» *Live Science,* April 27, 2017, https://www.livescience.com/58861-unified-field-theory.html.

[11] https://www.space.com/four-fundamental-forces.html.

[12] Strong's Concordance, «1411 dunamis," *Bible Hub,* https://biblehub.com/greek/1411.htm.

[13] J.I. Packer, *Praying the Lord's Prayer* (Wheaton, Illinois: Crossway, 2007), 108

[14] Strong's Concordance, «3519 kabowd," *Bible Hub,* https://biblehub.com/hebrew/3519.htm.

[15] *Vine's Complete Expository Dictionary* (Nashville: Thomas Nelson, 1996), 267.

[16] *ibid.*

[17] Strong's Concordance, "Mark 1:15," *Bible Hub,* https://biblehub.com/mark/1-15.htm.

[18] J. Dwight Pentecost, *Thy Kingdom Come* (Grand Rapids, Michigan: Kregel Publications: 1995), 14.

[19] John Piper, "What Is the Kingdom of God?" *Desiring God*, https://www.desiringgod.org/interviews/what-is-the-kingdom-of-god.

[20] "Quotable Quotes," *Good Reads*, https://www.goodreads.com/quotes/6439-if-we-find-ourselves-with-a-desire-that-nothing-in.

[21] Strong's Concordance, "165 aión," *Bible Hub,* https://biblehub.com/greek/165.htm.

[22] Vincenzo Dimonte, "The Real Meaning of To Infinity and Beyond!," *Cantor on the Shore,* October 21, 2014, http://cantorontheshore.blogspot.com/2014/10/the-real-meaning-of-to-infinity-and.html.

[23] https://www.firstthings.com/web-exclusives/2016/10/the-eternity-of-god.

[24] *Vine's Complete Expository Dictionary* (Nashville: Thomas Nelson, 1996), 72.

[25] C.H. Spurgeon, *The Treasury of David* (Grand Rapids, Michigan: Kregel Publications, 1976). 376.

WEEK 5 LIFESTYLE PRAYER

This, then, is how you should pray...
Matthew 6:9a

DAY 1 *CATYLIST*

"I'm just one guy, Lord. How can I help them? I don't have the time or money to make umpteen trips to Africa to lead conferences and work with worship leaders and pastors. I know they need help, but, really, what can I do? I'm just one person!"

Those words kept going through my head over and over for much of my return flight from Zambia, Africa, in 2015. We had just finished training over 400 leaders in 4 regions of that country. And now I couldn't shake the concern I felt for those I'd met. At all the conferences we led, worship leaders, worship teams and pastors alike packed the venues. They needed training and resources. But what could I do?

At the time I was the worship pastor at a church with over 2000 regular attenders in Louisville, Kentucky. I had a staff of 7 that I was responsible to lead, and my wife and I were busy trying to raise two teen-age boys. My plate was full, and I couldn't imagine taking on any more activities or ministry endeavors. Yet here I was on a 15-hour flight, and I was so burdened that I couldn't sleep on the plane or even watch movies! I kept thinking of the faces of those leaders as they would come up to us after the services. Clearly, they were hungry to learn and grow...

Sorry to interrupt the story. We will continue it in a moment. But first, I want to welcome you to our final week together in this study of the Model Prayer. Congratulations on getting this far! Over the past four weeks, we have broken the prayer apart, section by section and piece by piece. What an adventure of learning we have had! I encourage you to take some time to go back through the lessons, reading over your notes and highlights. It's important to remember those things that stood out to you and helped you the most.

This week the emphasis is on making the Model Prayer a *lifestyle* prayer. As we build a habit of praying and living out the Model Prayer each day, what sort of changes and challenges can we expect to experience? How could it affect our everyday activities and relationships? How might it impact our dreams and future? These are important questions we will address this week. I believe you will enjoy these next five lessons and grow through them. I know I have certainly grown through writing them!

Today's lesson includes a few personal stories to help paint a picture of the immense impact the Model Prayer has had on me. For years, I have tried to make a habit of applying the HE-WE-THEY approach to my daily prayers. I believe this has been a catalyst for much of the growth and fruit in my own life and in my family and ministry. Thank you for indulging me as I unpack some paradigm-changing moments I've had with the Lord!

Birth of a Dream

For hours during that plane ride back to Atlanta in 2015, I sat silently praying in my tiny airplane seat. I kept reminding myself that God is my Father in heaven and that I should submit to what he wants me to do (HE). (That part can be a struggle for me!) Time and again, I brought my concerns and burdens to the Lord (WE), and of course, I thought and prayed a lot for my new friends in Zambia (THEY). All in all, though, for the first 4 or 5 hours I mostly made excuses to God for why I couldn't help those leaders.

Then suddenly, the Lord's still, small voice broke through to my noisy and selfish heart. I sensed him whisper to me, "Dwayne, quit thinking *I*, and start thinking *we*." That was a paradigm shift of perspective for me, and it opened my mind to new possibilities I'd never considered before. The simple idea that came to me on the plane was to connect high-quality worship leaders we knew in the states with African worship leaders, to help mentor them and provide them with needed resources.

The thought of leaders helping leaders immediately arrested me.

That's a biblical idea! Even Jesus didn't try to teach every person himself; he poured into a few reliable men who then trained many others. Paul did the same thing in his ministry. I was so exhilarated by the idea of US/African sponsorships that I typed out the entire plan of how to go about it before I got off the plane that day!

When I got home, I immediately emailed a friend of mine in Zambia whom I'd been coaching in ministry. I wanted to know what he thought of the sponsorship idea. He loved it and began to help us move this God-sized dream forward.

To our knowledge no one had ever attempted something quite like this, so we found ourselves pioneering a new ministry approach. Nonetheless, we forged ahead with planning, and on the 13th of November 2015–exactly 6 months after the idea was birthed on that long plane ride–we launched our worship leader sponsorship program! We started with 10 trusted US sponsors paired with 10 eager Zambian leaders. We began getting great feedback on the personal friendships that were forming. The idea was working!

Permission

Although the sponsorships were going better than we'd expected, I sensed in my heart that God wanted us to do more. To be honest the thought intimidated me a little. I felt inadequate to do any more, and I felt a bit guilty allowing myself to dream such big dreams. Who did I think I was anyway? Those were the kinds of thoughts that kept running through my head.

I want to share with you now a quiet time I had in December of 2015. I journaled this devotional time about a month after we had launched the sponsorship program. It was very timely and encouraging. I titled this devotional "Permission to Dream Big for God."

The text for my quiet time that day was John 15:1-17. Please read that passage now. Be sure you stop and pray first and ask God to open your eyes to what he might want you to discover through it. What about this passage stands out to you right now? What can it teach you about prayer?

Below is what I wrote that morning in response to the passage in John 15. This is what I believe I heard God say from his written Word:

> Dwayne, when you stop dreaming you stop growing. When you cease to look ahead and take bold steps into new adventures

for God, you stop needing to rely as much on me; you stop stretching your faith. There is much more you could be doing and accomplishing to bear much more fruit for the kingdom. All you need do is ask for anything you want–anything, Dwayne–and it will be granted.

What I realized from his Word is that when we produce fruit, we are his true disciples. Why is that? It's simple. Much fruit requires much faith and love and brings much glory to God. Jesus produced much fruit, and as his followers, we should too. We should reach for more fruit. Step out into realms unknown. Step out of our boats, keeping our eyes fixed on Jesus. And whatever we do, do it all for his glory.

This is the response I wrote in my journal to what I saw in God's Word that morning.

Lord, for this season, I am convinced You are saying to me to launch out into deeper water, where I'll find a greater catch of fish, of people, to disciple for You. It's a daunting task, and one quite frankly I would rather run away from. Please help me, by Your grace, to accept this challenge from Your Spirit to boldly move into new areas of ministry.

Particularly, I'm thinking of the vision I believe You gave me to help provide worship discipleship materials and schools of training to worship leaders and pastors around the world. This would bring great glory to You. I have been called and prepared to do this. Thus, I will no longer wait around for You to nudge or push me forward. Precious holy Lord, grant me the grace, faith and deep abiding love for You and for others to now embrace my calling and move full steam ahead, trusting You to provide and guide.

As you can see, God lit a fire under me that day! I walked away from that amazing time in his Word with renewed boldness and faith. All my excuses had been stripped way. I shared the experience with my wife, Sonia. We prayed together and decided it was time to launch out into the deep and step out on faith.

Notice again how all 3 elements or parts of the Model Prayer were touched on in my response to God during that devotional. Honestly, I can't imagine praying to the Lord for very long without praising him and surrendering to him (HE), sharing my own needs and burdens (WE), and also praying for others (THEY).

With the help of some amazing friends and supporters, in April of 2016 we formed a non-profit, charitable ministry called Next Level Worship International, Inc. What a momentous time that was!

Ask Me

Fast forward to May of 2017. We had recently resigned from our church and gone full-time with NLW International. I had been home from Africa less than 24 hours when, after only a few hours of sleep, I woke early to a strong sense that God had something to say to me. So I got up and drove to our local city park.

Within minutes of getting to the park, I began to think about the Vine and branches that Jesus taught about. I knew the illustration came from John 15. So, I sat down at a picnic table and opened my Bible to that passage. The words that jumped out at me were in verses 7 and 16.

As I sat there fixated on those Scriptures, the Lord spoke clearly to my heart. He reminded me of how months earlier this same passage in John 15 had helped me see I had permission to dream big for his kingdom. I sensed him saying, "Dwayne, you've been dreaming huge things for your ministry, but you haven't been asking *me* for those things. Don't just dream–*ask*. You do not have, because you do not ask."

I admit that blew me away. It wasn't some "new" revelation; it had been in God's Word all along. I'd just never really seen it clearly before. It never felt so personal before. How much clearer does he need to be? Whatever we ask in his name the Father will give us. Wow, what a promise!

🧍 Go back and reread those verses in John 15, verses 7 and 16. What conditions do you see that we must meet in order to receive whatever we ask for?

My prayer journal is where I keep my "wish list" of prayer needs. Those requests include future hopes and dreams for our family and ministry. Some of them I share with our prayer partners and friends. Others, those I'm not ready to "go public" with yet, I keep private for my wife and me to ponder before the Lord.

Before we start asking God for any of the things on our wish list, we first try to be sure that whatever we wish for meets the prerequisites we see in John 15 and elsewhere in the Bible:

- Our wishes have to be God-given desires that he planted down inside us. Divinely inspired wishes only come from abiding in him and allowing his Word to abide in us.
- Our wishes have to be worthy of his name—things Jesus would approve of. Studying the Bible and confiding in godly counselors can help us discern those.
- Our dreams, if they came true, would need to help bring fruit for his kingdom. In order to qualify as his "whatever you ask for," the requests must have the potential to produce the fruit Jesus was talking about.
- Our wishes have to be things only God can do, so that only God can get glory for granting them.
- We would need to be determined to ask in faith and keep on asking—no matter how long it might take to receive an answer. As Jesus taught us about the persistent widow in Luke 18, God responds to our tenacity in prayer.

Incentive

I relied on the precepts of the Model Prayer as I worked through the process of discerning the Lord's will for our ministry. I want to share with you now some reasons why I think the Model Prayer can be used in any situation as a catalyst or "on-ramp" to help us grow and be more effective in God's kingdom.

God (HE) is who we consistently focus on in the Model Prayer by praising him, surrendering to his will and recognizing him as our heavenly Father. Doing this can melt away our fears and doubts and self-reliance. Our faith is increased as we meditate on his greatness and glory and praise him in spite of our circumstances.

By laying our cares down each day and entrusting concerns for ourselves and our family to the Lord, WE are then free to focus on the bigger world around us. Our peace and joy are restored, and our attitude moves from pessimism to God-focused optimism. We are then poised to think clearer, dream bigger and do more in the kingdom as he leads us.

When our eyes are lifted above our circumstances and concerns, we can then focus on others. THEY need our prayers and love. As we pray often for others, our burdens for them increase. We may be prompted to ask the Lord about other ways we can help them. Interceding for them can become a *catalyst* the Holy Spirit uses to move us to action.

Praying the Prayer

Take time to pray through each section of the Model Prayer now.

HE – Vertical

Praise and surrender to the God who has promised that if you "Stay joined to [him] and let [his] teachings become part of you, then you can pray for whatever you want and your prayer will be answered" (John 15: 7 CEV).

JOURNAL

WE – Personal

Write down some things that concern you right now. It could be a financial problem or issues at work or at home. Lay your burdens at Jesus' feet.

JOURNAL

THEY – Kingdom

Pray for someone besides you and your family. It might be your neighbor or someone you go to school or work with. Pray for other people's needs instead of your own now.

Review the prerequisites listed in this lesson that our petitions to God should meet. Now—what needs has God revealed to you which meet those criteria: requests for yourself, requests for people or situations near to your heart, and requests for others in God's kingdom?

JOURNAL

Living the Prayer

To be clear, break-through moments like the ones I've shared today are few and far between for me. Don't concern yourself with the big, mountain-top times. And certainly, don't compare your experiences with mine or anyone else's. Just be faithful and consistent each day to pray the prayer model and what it entails. Read and meditate on God's Word. The Lord will honor your faithfulness to focus on him. Trust that he is there with you, listening to you each and every time you call on him. As he promises in Psalm 91:15, "When they call on me, I will answer." You can take that promise to the bank!

DAY 2: CUE

As I am writing this, many parts of the US and the world are locked down because of COVID-19. According to a study from Barna Research, one in three practicing Christians has stopped attending church during the coronavirus pandemic. As this pandemic drags on into several months, there are growing concerns among pastors and church leaders that their congregants may get out of the habit of "going to church" and that many may not want to return once the COVID crisis subsides.

That may be the case for some Christians. However, I have hope many will return when they feel it safe to do so. I believe this for a couple of reasons: First, people who have experienced the rich rewards of meeting together face-to-face to fellowship and worship with other believers should yearn for that again. Secondly, many Christians have deep-set values and beliefs about the need to assemble with a local body of believers. Simply put, it's something they are convinced they are supposed to do.

The author of *Atomic Habits* says our system of actions is founded on our system of beliefs.[1] Like those for whom attending church is a given, what if we came to a place where we have a deep conviction about using the Lord's Prayer as a prayer model or template for our prayers? What if we really believed it is something God wants us to do? Our sincere beliefs about prayer could help keep us motivated to actually *pray*.

The Power of Habits

According to behavioral scientists, there is a three-step loop we all experience that helps us form habits. There are *cues* (or triggers) that lead to *routines* that lead to *rewards*. Over time, this loop of cue-routine-reward, cue-routine-reward becomes more and more automatic.[2]

Claude Hopkins understood this powerful reality about human nature, and he capitalized on it. Claude was an advertising magnate in the early 1900's. Many of the products he promoted became household names. Perhaps you've heard of Pepsodent toothpaste, for instance. Applying the three-step loop, Claude discovered he could persuade people to use his toothpaste over and over. He knew people wanted whiter teeth; so, he used that as the *cue* to cause them to buy his product. He told them the *routine* they needed for whiter teeth was to brush with it daily. And the *reward* he said they would receive was—you guessed it—whiter teeth. His strategy must have worked, for lots of people apparently formed a habit of using Pepsodent. They sold tons of the stuff![3]

I use the illustration of Pepsodent to help us understand how habits are formed and what steps are involved. Obviously, my motive is not to get you to buy a certain toothpaste or to have whiter teeth. What we will address today is far more important than mere cosmetic improvements. I'm not the least bit interested in whether you have a routine of brushing your teeth (although for your loved ones' sakes I hope you do!). The routine to impact all other routines in life is praying the pattern of the Lord's Prayer. We've invested the past four weeks learning about and practicing that routine. Today we need to examine what lies on each side of the routine in the habit loop–its cues and rewards.

What Cues You?

Early in our Christian lives, most of us recited the Lord's Prayer only when asked to do so by another person, perhaps by a parent or a pastor or teacher. Even if you were already in the habit of saying it in your personal prayer times, I'm guessing you weren't praying it as a pattern of HE, WE, THEY until you went through this study. These lessons, like people, can serve as external cues for us. Our study is coming to a close, however. Does that mean you will cease to pray through this pattern on your own? Will you do it even though you are no longer being cued from an outside source?

Here is why it matters. Say that your house is on fire. Okay, I know that is a terrible and unwelcome thought, but horrifying moments like that can occur. What would be your first thought if it suddenly happened to you? Many would freak-out at the sight of their house on fire. Some might even have a mental meltdown because of it. Such reactions are natural and understandable for a person who doesn't know Christ. But we do know him. He is our Father and Lord. Our response to crises should reflect our deep faith in God.

What if we had conditioned ourselves to think differently when a crisis hits us? What if we'd already been preparing ourselves by praying the elements of the prayer model each day and conditioning our mind with the truth of God's Word? How might it affect our attitude and response if, in that split second when we realized the danger, we were to mentally pause and run a quick *checklist based on the Model Prayer*?

- Father, you are still on the throne. I trust you. I surrender to your will. (HE)
- Here are my pressing needs and fears right now. Please help me. (WE)
- How can you be glorified through this? How can I be your witness? (THEY)

The cue we need in order to trigger the routine of praying the Model Prayer in each and every circumstance is a deep-set *conviction* that it matters and that Jesus said to "pray like this."

Present

In order to form a lasting habit, we need more than a cue and a routine. Experts tell us we also need a reward. Good news is that there are several rewards for praying the Model Prayer each day! Let's look at a few.

Read through the Lord's Prayer now. Highlight every statement that is in the present tense—that refers to the here and now.

As we meditate on the Model Prayer and internalize it, incorporating it within our minds and hearts, it will help us *live in the present.* The only reference to the past in the Lord's Prayer is, "Forgive us our debts." Once we have confessed any known sins, we never need to bring them up again. So, we don't have to dwell on the past. "He has removed our sins as far from us as the east is from the west" (Psalm 103:12). We are forgiven!

We should pray for his will to be done on earth. That's a wonderful, futuristic idea. But then we are immediately brought back to the present in the very next phrase of the prayer: "as it *is* in heaven." We can't control the future. We can pray for it and anticipate it, but we can't regulate it, and we shouldn't worry about it. After all, yesterday is gone, and tomorrow will never come. All we really have is today. We have to trust God and make the most of today. We must live in the moment and "make every minute count" (Ephesians 5:16 CEV).

Priorities

Internalizing the Model Prayer is also rewarding because it helps us *align our priorities.*

Read through the Model Prayer again. Look closely. What does Jesus *not* mention in his model of prayer? What is noticeably missing?

What I want us to see is that there is no reference to us *doing* anything in the Lord's Prayer. Did you catch that? Imagine that. This is the mother of all prayers, if you will, and the model we are to follow. Yet, it makes no mention of doing stuff for God.

Wouldn't it make sense for Jesus to have included a request like, "Help us do great feats"? After all, shouldn't we want to do great things for the Lord? Absolutely. Daniel 11:32 says, "The people who know their God shall be strong and carry out great exploits" (NKJV). The problem comes when we let *doing* take priority over *being*. Notice it says the people who *know their God*. Those are the ones who will do great exploits. The prerequisite for doing is *knowing* and *being*.

There are no requests in the Model Prayer to amass wealth or make great conquests. No mention of doing events or programs. The Model Prayer doesn't ask for help to succeed in business or build a big church or ministry. The only reference in the Lord's Prayer to us doing anything is forgiving others. Yet even that is not an outward activity; it is an inward attitude. *The Lord's Prayer is a prayer of the heart for the heart.* What a revelation! Could it be that too many of our prayers are activity-focused or project-focused rather than God-focused? Could it be that we are not to spend as much time asking for outward things, but rather to seek inward change for ourselves and others?

♪ Paul focused on inward change when he prayed for the Ephesian church. Underline every reference Paul makes to the inner person in this passage: "I pray that from his glorious, unlimited resources he will empower you with inner strength through his Spirit. Then Christ will make his home in your hearts as you trust in him. Your roots will grow down into God's love and keep you strong. And may you have the power to understand, as all God's people should, how wide, how long, how high, and how deep his love is. May you experience the love of Christ, though it is too great to understand fully. Then you will be made complete with all the fullness of life and power that comes from God" (Ephesians 3:16-19).

♪ Now read John 17:20-26. This is Jesus' famous prayer for all believers. Notice that he makes no requests for us to *do* things for the Father. Everything he prays for us has to do with who we *are*, not with what we do.

As the Lord's Prayer and its elements of HE, WE and THEY become woven into our daily lives, we will encounter the Father and get to know him in ways we never dreamed possible. As one commentator put it, "To seek the face of the Lord is…to enjoy his gracious presence, and the light of his countenance…It is to seek the Lord himself, and have communion with him through Christ, the brightness of his glory."[4]

Peace

Perhaps the most incredible reward that comes along with praying the Lord's prayer as a habit in our lives is *lasting peace*. This peace comes from knowing, trusting, and worshiping God.

The HE section of the Model Prayer reminds us of the necessity of a relationship with "our Father." To know God is to know peace. Romans 5:1 says, "Therefore, since we have been made right in God's sight by faith, we have peace with God because of what Jesus Christ our Lord has done for us." Because our sins are forgiven and we have been made right in his eyes, we have peace through his Son. When we harbor sin in our hearts and we fail to confess, then that hinders our peace with God as well as our prayers.

The WE section is where we lay our needs and burdens before him. We can trust him to forgive our sins and not hold our debts against us. We trust him to walk with us through the evil times of life. As a young child trusts his parent, so we can fully trust our trust-worthy Father. Isaiah said, "You keep him in perfect peace whose mind is stayed on you, because he trusts in you" (26:3 ESV).

The THEY section of the Prayer climaxes with exuberant praise. Praying to our awesome God can warm our hearts with peace that leads to praise. If you read my book *Hearing God Say Well Done*, then you may recall a story I shared about Jason Beam and his family. Their son, Tucker, went through three cancers, finally succumbing to the last one, leukemia, and dying at nine years of age. I'll never forget at the funeral that it was Jason who stood first and started praising God. He raised his hands high and worshiped the Lord passionately among the thousand people gathered there. That day, some 40 doctors, nurses and others surrendered their lives to Christ.

Recently, Jason's youngest daughter Lily was diagnosed with cancer on her 13th birthday. Like Tucker, Lily has leukemia. This is the 9th cancer diagnosis among their immediate family. Many, including my family, watched to see how Jason would respond and what he would say to the jolting news of her diagnosis. Most of us would be tempted to be angry at God, but Jason and his wife, Courtney, are unusual. They have a deep, deep faith. They know and trust their God. Here's what Jason said in his first tweet when he announced it: "We are broken-hearted for our amazing daughter and wish we could take this all away completely. But we can't, and now this is the next fight we have before us. We lean on our faith and trust in Jesus to walk with us through this."

How in the world can someone be that calm and assured? How is that possible? It's only possible because of the sustaining *peace* that comes when we put our faith and trust in Christ, and we lay our needs before him. That's what praying the Lord's Prayer can do. It can build our most holy faith as we lay our every need before the Father and worship him every day.

Clearly for the Beam family, prayer is far more than mental consent to an ancient prayer spoken at church services and weddings. Prayer is a deep-set habit and conviction in their lives. May we all possess such a deep belief in prayer. And may that conviction cue us each and every day to pray the Model Prayer as Jesus said to pray.

Praying the Prayer

Take time to pray and journal through each section of the Model Prayer now.

HE – Vertical

As you worship and surrender yourself to God today, you may want to appropriate Paul's prayer for the church in Ephesians 3 making it your own: "Lord, I pray that, from your glorious, unlimited resources, you will empower me with inner strength through your spirit. May Christ make his home in my heart as I trust in him. I pray that my roots will grow down into God's love and keep me strong. Grant me the power to understand, as all God's people should, how wide, how long, how high, and how deep his love is. Please help me to experience the love of Christ, though it is too great to understand fully. Allow me to be made complete with all the fullness of life and power that comes from God."

JOURNAL

WE – Personal

Do you have Christian loved ones for whom you could pray this prayer, substituting their names for *you* and *your*? Lift to God other prayer requests you have.

JOURNAL

THEY – Kingdom

Pray for others who need to experience the love of Christ and situations that require his touch.

Review the prerequisites listed in Day 1 of this week that our petitions to God should meet. Now—what needs has God revealed to you which meet those criteria: requests for yourself, requests for people or situations near to your heart, and requests for others in God's kingdom?

JOURNAL

Living the Prayer

Review the checklist under the "What Cues You?" portion of this lesson. Throughout your day today or tomorrow, run that checklist in your mind whenever you are faced with a situation or circumstance you need help with. Deliberately apply the pattern of the Model Prayer to every decision and situation you face.

DAY 3: *CACOPHONY*

In his book, *Moving Mountains*, John Eldridge spoke for many of us when he wrote, "Often when we first turn to prayer, we are coming out of the Matrix–that whirling, suffocating Mardi Gras of this world–and it takes some time to calm down and turn our gaze on him."[5]

One might call this unsettling disturbance *cacophony*, which is defined as a "a harsh discordant mixture of sounds."[6] An example of cacophony in everyday life would be the combination of different sounds in a busy city street or a market—vehicles, announcements on loudspeakers, music, chatter of people, dogs barking—all at the same time and without any harmony.

In our spiritual lives, there is a constant and seemingly endless cacophony of distractions we must deal with. A more common word for what we often endure is *noise*. Noise can come from things around us, but it can also come from cluttered thoughts inside us. If we are not careful, both sources can have a hindering, even devastating, effect on our prayer lives.

What do most people do when they hear obnoxious noises? They turn down the volume or roll up the window or put in ear plugs. There are several ways to deal with physical noises. Fortunately, there are also some things we can do to decrease the noises—whether literal or metaphorical—that we experience as Christians. To maintain a lifestyle of worship and prayer, it is vital we learn to overcome them.

Noise around us

"Our attention can be mined. We are more profitable to a corporation if we're spending time staring at a screen, staring at an ad, than if we're spending that time living our lives in a rich way. And so we're seeing the results of that. We're seeing corporations using powerful artificial intelligence to outsmart us and to figure out how to pull our attention toward the things they want us to look at rather than the things that are most consistent with our goals, and our values and our lives."[7]

That quote is from a recent documentary titled *The Social Dilemma*. The guy who said that is Justin Rosenstein, a former engineer at Facebook and Google. What he is referring to is something you and I are probably too familiar with: social media.

I can't tell you how many times I've been pulled away from my flow of thoughts and prayers or from reading the Bible or some wholesome book by an annoying alert on my phone. It might as well be screaming at me that I have a message and I need to check it. Can you relate? I use an app on my iPad to read the Bible each morning, which is very convenient. Problem is, that device is connected to the internet, so it's distracting me every time I get a like or a happy face on Facebook!

Tips to decrease the noise of social media:

- During your quiet times, turn down the audio alerts and flip over your phone so you can't see visible alerts.
- Try to avoid getting on social media or posting anything on your social media apps before your prayer times. The most common time to get likes and responses is in the minutes right after you post something.
- Use a paper-printed Bible rather than reading it electronically and journal in a paper notebook if needed to avoid using your devices.

If those ideas don't work, you might need to go cold-turkey! Consider deleting your social media apps and turning off notifications for a few days or weeks.

Allowing ourselves to be distracted by life's constant demands on our attention can result in the neglect of the most important priorities: loving God and others. In the book of Revelation, Jesus gave a serious indictment against the Church at Ephesus. He said, "I know all the things you do. I have seen your hard work and your patient endurance. I know you don't tolerate evil people. You have examined the claims of those who say they are apostles but are not. You have discovered they are liars. You have patiently suffered for me without quitting. But I have this complaint against you. You don't love me or each other as you did at first!" (Revelation 2:2-4).

Apparently, the Ephesian church was so busy doing the work of ministry that they failed to make time to stay in love with God and his people. Busyness in ministry can make us feel good about ourselves. But the Lord is more interested in the condition of our hearts and our fellowship with him.

🎵 Read the account of Martha and Mary in Luke 10:38-42. Who welcomed Jesus? Who worked for Jesus? Who worshiped Jesus? Which person did Jesus recognize and honor?

If you're like me, you know you need to make a priority of seeking God and praying. For so long though, I just didn't quite know how to do it. I struggled to manage my time well. Then I discovered a book called *First Things First* by Stephen Covey. It helped me organize my activities into quadrants.

Basically, there are four quadrants that our "to-do" items can be placed in. In the first quadrant (Q1) are activities that are important and urgent, like fixing a leaky pipe or stopping for fuel when your vehicle is running low. In the second quadrant (Q2) are activities that are important but not urgent, such as reading the Bible or playing a board game with your family. The third quadrant (Q3) consists of items that are urgent but not important, and the fourth (Q4), those which are neither urgent nor important.

The idea is very simple. Write out your to-do list for the week, and then identify which quadrant each item is in. Schedule Quadrant 2 items in advance and be sure to prioritize them on your schedule. For example, in the case of time for prayer and meditation on the Word, place that as a Q2 on your daily calendar. Then, be sure to do it *before* you do the activities listed in other quadrants (unless it's an emergency Q1).

Much can be said about this topic of busyness. Whole books have been written about being overly busy in ministry and in life. No doubt that's because so many of us struggle with it! It is certainly not something you or I can conquer in a day or a month. But in time and by God's grace, we can improve in this vital area of prioritizing our love for and time with God.

Tips to decrease the noise of busyness:
- Faithfully utilize the quadrant system of time management and work at prioritizing what is most important but not urgent.
- Ask someone to hold you accountable to better manage your time each week and prioritize time with God to pray and seek him.
- Slow down your pace and rest more. Meditate on Scriptures that

remind you it is God's ministry, and trust that he can get the job done even without you.

Another noise to beware of is misguided philosophies about prayer. According to studies, the coronavirus pandemic has ramped up people's prayer lives. Many are turning to it. Web searches on prayer are increasing on all continents for both Christians and Muslims, even in Denmark, one of the least religious countries in the world.[8] The question is, to whom are they praying?

As I write this lesson I am in the mountains of North Georgia. Yesterday I ate lunch at a local restaurant. When I told the waitress I was in town on a writing retreat, she asked me what I was writing about. I told her I was writing a study on prayer, and she immediately responded, "Oh good. People need to pray. Praying is important." I replied, "Yes, it is." Then she said, "People need to feel good about themselves. They need to know they have light inside them. Prayer can help them discover themselves." At that moment I realized that young lady had no idea what prayer is really about.

Unfortunately, she is not alone. Many people are confused about prayer. They don't know whom they should pray to or why. Lots of folks only pray for what they can get out of God. They are unwilling to submit to him and to his commandments and will. Others see prayer and meditation as a means of self-help and self-care. They may not even be praying to the God of the Bible, the one true God. Some people would have us believe we don't need to pray the "old-fashioned way." They want us to utilize their so-called modern techniques of meditation and embrace their "enlightened" alternatives to prayer. Don't fall for that!

Tips to decrease the noise of false teachings and philosophies:
- Trust the teaching you have received from godly mentors. More importantly, trust what God's Word says about prayer and do what you know to be correct and true based on the Bible.
- Quit allowing yourself to be influenced by people with strange notions about prayer and following God.
- Pray often and go deep in your personal connection with God in prayer. As A.W. Tozer said, "True prayer cannot be imitated, nor can it be learned from [anyone]…but the Holy Spirit."[9]

Noise within us

Sometimes the distractions we hear inside us can be louder than those from other people and places. Take doubt and discouragement, for example. Think about times you've been loaded down with worry. Have you ever been so discouraged that you wondered if God was even listening to your prayers? In times like that, the noise of doubt and despair can drown out his still, small voice of love and compassion. It's ironic actually. I say ironic because a major purpose of prayer is to give God our worries. Yet sometimes, our minds are so full of worry that we can't offer to God our prayers. We can't focus on anything but that which is weighing us down.

Tips to decrease the noise of doubt and discouragement:

- Be honest with God. He already knows what you are thinking anyway. He can handle your emotions and doubts when you bring them to him in humble prayer. As one author wrote, "Honest dealing becomes us when we kneel in His pure presence."[10]
- Identify your source of discouragement. By isolating that, you may discover your hope was in the wrong person or in the wrong goal or idea.
- Preach to yourself. Meditate on Scriptures about worry and doubt.
- Choose to believe God over your emotions or logic. Praise him despite your feelings. Ask him to comfort you and give you "the oil of joy instead of mourning, and a garment of praise instead of a spirit of despair" (Isaiah 61:3).

Temptation is another noise we contend with. In Week 3 Day 5 we talked about the three sources of temptation: the world, the flesh, and the devil. Today I want to home in on our thought-life, for it is in our minds that tempting thoughts can take root, enticing us to sin (James 1:14). Our thoughts can also lead us toward prayer or away from it. Ultimately it is our thoughts that lead us closer to God or farther away from him.

Proverbs 4:23 says, "Guard your heart above all else, for it determines the course of your life." To guard our hearts means we must guard our minds and thoughts. So, the question we need to ask ourselves is, what kind of thoughts are we thinking? Quoting Tozer again, "Anyone who wishes to check on his true spiritual condition may do so by noting what his voluntary thoughts have been over the last hours or days."[11]

    ♫   Read 1 Timothy 6:7-10. According to Paul, what love is the root of all evil? How might that love pull us away from a pure love for Christ? How do you think that craving could affect our worship and our prayer life?

Jesus said in Luke 16:13, "No one can serve two masters. Either you will hate the one and love the other, or you will be devoted to the one and despise the other. You cannot serve both God and money" (NIV). Another way to say that is, you can't *worship* God and money. If we aren't careful, we can care more for money than we do for God. A desire for wealth or other things can become an idol in our lives, and when it does, our worship of the Lord as well as our prayers to him will go down the drain. Oh, we may keep praying, but he will not hear us. He will allow no other gods before him (Exodus 20:3).

Once our thoughts have turned to that which tempts us and we allow it to lead us to sin, then the noise we experience inside our hearts becomes our own. It is of our own making. And it is the worst noise of all, for it shuts down our communion with God. Those times of sweet fellowship in prayer, those spontaneous moments of praise, the comfort and peace we have enjoyed in knowing he was walking with us every day and guiding us–it all evaporates the second we disobey him and turn to worship our idol.

Isaiah 59:2 gives us a somber warning: "It's your sins that have cut you off from God. Because of your sins, he has turned away and will not listen anymore." *The only way we can "turn down" the noise of sin in our hearts is to repent.*

Living the Prayer

In 2 Chronicles 7:14, God told the Israelites, "If my people who are called by my name humble themselves and pray and seek my face and turn from their wicked ways, then I will hear from heaven and will forgive their sin and heal their land." That same promise can be applied to us today. What do you need to repent of? Do you have any unconfessed sins you've been harboring? If you have already confessed them to the Lord, then they are forgiven and forgotten by him. But if you have not, then do it right now. Don't wait another minute to make things right between you and the Lord. Trust him to hear you, forgive you, and to immediately restore you to unbroken fellowship with him.

Take time to pray through and journal each section of the Model Prayer now.

HE – Vertical
Use some of the tips in this lesson to block out the cacophony of the world and give 100% of your attention to the Savior who gave 100% of himself for you! A good song to listen to as you worship and surrender yourself to God is Marie Barnett's "Breathe":

> "This is the air I breathe..., Your holy presence living in me. This is my daily bread..., Your very word spoken to me. And I, I'm desperate for you. And I, I'm lost without you."[12]   When we become desperate for God and feel lost away from his presence, the noises of our world just fade away.

WE – Personal
After your time of worship and surrender, ask the Lord to speak to you about whom and what you should pray for—both those in your immediate circle and those outside it. Then be silent and listen to his answer. Then PRAY, pouring out your heart to him.

JOURNAL

THEY – Kingdom
Pray for someone besides you and your family. It might be your neighbor or someone you go to school or work with. Pray for other people's needs instead of your own now.

JOURNAL

DAY 4: COMMUNE

To commune with someone is "to be in intimate communication, to converse or talk together, usually with profound intensity and intimacy."[13] Communing with God is vital to our prayer life for two reasons. First, we need to be in communion with God before we can pray effectively. Conversely, as we pray in communion with God each day, it can actually enhance or intensify communion and intimacy with the Lord.

🕊 Read the following passages in Matthew. They are 5:3-11, 6:5-14, 6:25-34, and 7:7-11. How might what Jesus said in these verses relate to prayer?

The word "commune" is not actually in the Sermon on the Mount. Nonetheless, if we look closer, we can discover some exciting clues to help us see the importance of communing with God through prayer.

Clue 1: God wants to be involved in our lives.

The first clue that we see in the Sermon is in the "Be-attitudes," as they are sometimes called. God blesses certain people for certain things. For example, God blesses the humble and the peacemakers and those going through persecution for his sake. He blesses each of them specifically. To bless us individually means that he knows who we are. As Dr. Adrian Rogers once said, "Everybody has God all to himself. In fact, God doesn't love us all; He loves us each."[14] The personal attention God gives us paves the way for close fellowship and communion between us. Since it's important to him, it should be important to us.

Clue 2: He is our Father.

Because he cares so deeply for us and wants to be involved in our lives, he made a way to be our forever Father through his Son, Jesus Christ. 1 John 4:19 says, "We love him because he first loved us." He is our God; yet he's more than that to us. He's not just the Father. He is *our* Father. And that small possessive adjective, *our,* makes all the difference in the ability and privilege we have to commune with him in prayer. (Hallelujah!)

Clue 3: He wants to grant our requests.

The third clue to the importance of communion is found in chapter 7. If we were to take that passage out of its context, it might sound as though

Jesus was promising that anyone could ask anything of God and he or she would receive it. But we must be careful to read passages in relation to the verses that surround them. When we do, we see that Jesus is referring to those who have a *relationship* with God. We're not speaking to a stranger when we pray. We are communing with our Abba Father. (Wow!)

To understand even better how this clue relates to the importance of communing with God, we need to look at John 15. There Jesus enlightens us on exactly who has the opportunity to ask and receive from the Lord. John 15:7 says, "If you abide in me, and my words abide in you, ask whatever you wish, and it will be done for you" (ESV). Therefore, we can only ask and receive if we are abiding in him. *To abide* can be defined as to continue, endure, last, live, and remain.[15] Abiding includes the idea of communing. Only as we abide and commune with God can we enjoy the powerful promise of receiving what we ask for.

When we combine all three of these clues, it makes for a pretty convincing argument that communion with God matters when we pray. It definitely matters when we pray the Lord's Prayer. Think about it: We can call on his name because he knows our name. We have the right to speak to him as his children because he is our Father. And finally, we can boldly ask for the things we need because we abide in him and he in us.

Results

Now that we understand how vital communion is to effectively praying the Lord's Prayer, let's look on the other side of that. How can praying the Lord's Prayer in turn enhance our communion?

Benefit 1: We are compelled to go deeper in our communication with God.

In his book, *Why Am I Afraid to Tell You Who I Am?* John Powell describes five levels of communication and how people relate to one another. We can apply these levels to our communication with God.

- Level Five is what he calls "Cliche Conversation." This level of communication consists of shallow conversations.
- Level Four is "Reports Facts About the Other." Little real communication happens on this level. People talk about others but expose almost nothing about themselves.

159

- Level Three is "My Ideas and Judgments." On this level there starts to be some real communication. Individuals begin to communicate their ideas, opinions and decisions, although communication tends to remain guarded.
- Level Two is "My Feelings (or emotions)." Communication on this level includes individuals sharing what is going on inside them and how they feel about a certain situation, experience or person. Powell says, "Most feel that others will not tolerate such emotional honesty in communication…[so] we settle for superficial relationships."[16]
- Level One is Peak Communication. This kind of communication takes place in deep and authentic relationships where a person is emotionally open and honest with the other person. According to Powell, "At these times the two will feel an almost perfect and mutual empathy."[17]

A great example of Peak Communication is the relationship between Moses and God. Read Exodus 32 and 33 now. This is more reading than I usually ask you to do. But it's needed in order to better grasp the deep relationship and communication between Moses and the Lord.

Did you notice how it described their relationship in chapter 33:11? It says, "…the LORD would speak to Moses face to face, as one speaks to a friend." We shouldn't assume we understand what the Bible means by the phrase "as one speaks to a friend." Let's face it, few friendships nowadays go deeper than level 4. Most of us prefer to talk about the weather, or where we went shopping, or what we watched on TV last night. We wouldn't think of divulging personal information to most of our so-called friends.

What does the writer of Exodus mean when he gives that description of God's communication with Moses in Exodus 33:11? The Hebrew word used for *speak* is also found in Exodus 25. In that chapter God was instructing Moses on how to build the ark of the covenant for the tabernacle. In verse 22, he said to Moses, "There, above the cover between the two cherubim that are over the ark of the covenant law, I will meet with you and give you all my commands for the Israelites." When God spoke to Moses, it wasn't just chit-chat. He met with Moses for a purpose. In Exodus 25, he said he would speak to Moses to give him all his commands for his people. The conversation in Exodus 33 had a purpose as well: to discuss God's accompanying Moses and the Israelites to the Promised Land.

When we approach God and talk with him, we should never approach him like we are just hanging out with a pal. We should reverently treat him as our holy, heavenly Father who is also our Friend. Praying the prayer model opens the door for us to meet with our Father and hear from him and communicate with him on a deep level.

In Exodus 33, God allowed Moses to have a glimpse of his infinite glory. We can't even begin to imagine how awesome that moment must have been for Moses. It so impacted him that it literally made him glow with God's presence, and the glow was so bright that he had to put a veil over his face when he talked to people (Exodus 34:33)! All of that happened because of the raw and open communion Moses and God had with each other. That is the kind of communication God wants to have with us. Granted, we may never reach the level of intimacy Moses enjoyed with the Lord, but we too can get to know our God and enjoy his presence.

Benefit 2: We are challenged to commune with God in our everyday activities.

As praying the Model Prayer becomes our lifestyle, we'll find ways to apply it and do it every day and in every place. It will become a part of who we are. Because of this, we will also begin to experience greater communion with God in our everyday lives–whether at work, school, home, or play.

Brother Lawrence was a humble cook. Although he lived in the 1600's, his close walk with the Lord continues to challenge believers today. In *The Practice of the Presence of God,* his biographer wrote this about him: "The set times of prayer were no different for him than other times. He secluded himself to pray, according to the directions of his Superior. But he did not need such solitude, nor did he ask for it. Even the busiest work did not distract him from his communion with God." Brother Lawrence believed that "In order to form a habit of communing with God continually and committing everything we do to Him, we must at first make a special effort. After a while we find that His love inwardly inspires us to do all things for Him effortlessly."[18]

Brother Lawrence saw his walk with God and his communion with

God as a 24-hours-a-day thing and something he enjoyed 7 days a week. So it should be with us. Deliberately praying each element of the Model Prayer is a wonderful way to "make a special effort" to commune with our precious Lord.

Benefit 3: We are encouraged to pray freely and creatively.
The third way praying the Lord's Prayer enhances our communion with God is that it helps us see there is not one set way to pray. I realize that may sound like it is going against what we have been saying in this study. I think there are rich benefits to praying the Model Prayer in the way we have laid it out here. One element certainly leads to the next, as we tried to point out in Week 1. Still, I don't believe we are *commanded* to pray in that particular order. There should be great freedom of expression in our conversations with our best Friend!

Here is the "elephant in the room" question that we haven't addressed yet. If the pattern of the Lord's Prayer is really that important, then why don't we see other prayers in the Bible follow that order? That is a great question that deserves an answer. While it is true there aren't other prayers that follow that exact pattern, all the prayers of the Bible have at least one of the Prayer's elements within them.

We need to do more than simply examine each prayer individually. We need to zoom out and consider other prayers by that same individual. Take Paul, for example. Did Paul ever praise God and surrender to him in his prayers? Absolutely. The entire first chapter of Ephesians is a prayer "to the praise of his glory." Did Paul pray for himself? Certainly. He prayed for his thorn in the flesh to be removed in 2 Corinthians 12. Did he intercede for others? Yes, many times! In fact, we read earlier this week how Paul passionately interceded for the Church at Ephesus. Although we don't have a transcription of Paul praying all three elements in the same recorded prayer, he certainly had a *lifestyle* of prayer which included all of them.

Beyond reciting certain words, the Model Prayer is really more of a mindset and a deep matter of the heart. Paul said we should "pray without ceasing" (1 Thessalonians 5:17). Thus, you might think of the Lord's Prayer as a *continuous prayer* you pray all day long. You might start with praise and surrender in the morning. Then later in the day, you may feel burdened to pray for yourself and your loved ones. Then, at another time, perhaps you stop and pray for other people like your neighbors and co-workers. In that scenario, you still include all three elements in your day;

you just pray them at different times of your day.

The issue isn't whether we always pray Jesus' prayer model in a certain ordered pattern. The problem happens when we fail to intentionally include all three elements in our daily life of prayer. We can get out of focus as Christians if we don't include praise and surrender (HE), petitions (WE) and intercessions (THEY).

That is why I try to pray the pattern of the Lord's Prayer at least once a day. I usually begin my day on my knees going through each of the elements. It is a powerfully humbling time as I focus on my Father, lay out my burdens, and pray for others. It helps me prepare my mind and heart for whatever may come in my day ahead.

Praying the Prayer

I encourage you to take some time to praise and pray through this "expanded" version of the Lord's Prayer by John Calvin. Enjoy!

Our Father — Who art good and gracious to all, our Creator, our Preserver; the Father of our Lord, and of us in him, thy children by adoption and grace:...the Father of the universe, of angels and men:

Who art in heaven — the almighty Lord and Ruler of all...in heaven – Eminently there, but not there alone, seeing thou fillest heaven and earth.

Hallowed be thy name — Mayest thou, O Father, be truly known by all intelligent beings,...mayest thou be duly honoured, loved, feared, by all in heaven and in earth, by all angels and all men.

Thy kingdom come — May thy kingdom of grace come quickly and... may all mankind, receiving thee, O Christ, for their king, truly believing in thy name, be filled with righteousness, and peace, and joy; with holiness and happiness, till they are removed...into thy kingdom of glory, to reign with thee for ever and ever.

Thy will be done on earth, as it is in heaven — May all the inhabitants of the earth do thy will as willingly as the holy angels;...mayest thou,... through the blood of the everlasting covenant, make them perfect in every good work to do thy will, ...

Give us — O Father...*this day* - (for we take no thought for the morrow) *our daily bread* – All things needful for our souls and bodies... and thy grace, the food which endureth to everlasting life.

And forgive us our debts, as we also forgive our debtors — Give us,

O Lord, redemption in thy blood, even the forgiveness of sins: as thou enablest us freely and fully to forgive every man, so do thou forgive all our trespasses.

And lead us not into temptation but deliver us from evil — Whenever we are tempted… [allow] us not to enter into temptation;…but make a way for us to escape, so that we may be more than conquerors, through thy love, over sin and all the consequences of it.

For thine is the kingdom — The sovereign right of all things that are or ever were created: The power…whereby thou governest all things in thy everlasting kingdom: And the glory – The praise due from every creature, for thy power, and all thy wondrous works, and the mightiness of thy kingdom, which endureth through all ages, even for ever and ever.

Living the Prayer

S.M. Lockridge once said, "Every one of us has a check made out on the bank of heaven, but many of us fail to cash it at the window of prayer. Prayer is man's job. That's the only unending obligation that our Lord has given to men. He did not say that men ought to always work. He did not say that men ought to always play. But he said men ought to always pray."[19]

Pray today as if your life depended on it.

JOURNAL

DAY 5: *CHOICE*

Today is our last lesson together. We've had an incredible experience. Thank you so much for sticking with it to the end. I hope this is actually just the *beginning* of a lifestyle of prayer that you continue to grow in.

I suggest you take time to go back through the book and review your notes. Highlight things that stood out to you and that you want to be sure to remember and take away from this study. Celebrate what the Lord has taught you. It will help you solidify what you've learned. Also, *please go to www.prayermodel.com and tell us about your experience with the study and how it helped you.* You can leave us prayer requests and connect with others in our global community at NLW International.

The ultimate goal of this study has been to help you grow as a worshiper of the Most High God. Nothing is more vital in your life and in mine than to worship the Lord in spirit and in truth. The HE portion of the Lord's Prayer helps us *adore God* and love him more. The WE section leads us to *abide in him* for our needs, and the final section, THEY, should prompt us to *attend to others* by helping them and sharing Christ' love with them. Those three things–adoring, abiding, and attending–sum up the essence of whole-life worship. The Model Prayer–when used as a prayer model–is a powerful tool to help accomplish the lofty and noble goal of being a life-long worshiper.

Matter of the Heart

As we pray the prayer model, it can shape our heart for worship. But what is a "heart for worship" exactly? What does it look like? In order to help develop a worshiping heart in ourselves and in others, we should have a clear understanding of the kind of heart that's needed to worship God.

As we have already seen earlier in our study, worship is really a matter of the heart. True worship begins on the inside of us with loving God and others deeply. But since it's on the inside, we can't see it. Therefore, we can't give a clear, visual description of how a heart for worship looks. Not only that, but we also can't look at someone and immediately know if that person has a heart for worship. While we can't actually see a heart for worship, there are certain characteristics those with worshiping hearts have in common.

♫ Psalm 51 is David's psalm of repentance for his sins of adultery and murder. How David approached God and what he prayed in Psalm 51 demonstrates his humble heart for worship. Read that psalm now. What does David say that might lead you to believe he loved God and wanted to honor him?

Reading through the many psalms King David wrote, it is quite clear he had a deep and abiding faith in God. He knew his God well, for he had invested many days and nights with the Lord out in the fields and under the stars as a shepherd boy. Because of its rich instruction, Psalm 51 has been called "the brightest gem in the whole Book [of Psalms]."[20] This powerfully transparent psalm reveals some important qualities of God-worshipers. Let's look at those.

Clean

David prayed earnestly for God to create in him a clean heart (Ps. 51:10). Believers with hearts for worship desire to be clean before God. They are done with dirty living. They enjoy the peace forgiveness brings, and they never want to go back to their old lives again. They long to be in God's presence, communing freely with him. They are miserable when their sin separates them from fellowship with their heavenly Father. Simply put, they love and prefer to worship and please the Lord.

Although a person with a heart for worship may occasionally sin, he or she repents quickly and turns back to God. When David was confronted by the prophet Nathan about his sin in 2 Samuel 12, he admitted it right there on the spot. As C.H. Spurgeon explains, David "was a man of very strong passions, a soldier, and an Oriental monarch. No other king of his time would have felt any [guilt] for having [sinned] as he did."[21] But David wasn't like any other king of his time. He was a worshiper. And after a brief season of trying to cover up his transgressions, he chose repentance.

Constant

In the same breath with "Create in me a pure heart, O God" in verse 10, David also prays, "Renew a steadfast spirit within me." Those two ideas go hand in hand with a worshiper. David didn't just want to get clean. He wanted to *stay* clean. The Hebrew word for steadfast means "to be firm, stable, established, securely determined."[22] David desired constancy in his life, so he would not fall again into sin and so he would always follow God's commandments.

A worshiper's life should be marked with consistency. Why is that? It's because God is consistent. God never changes. Gazing on his never-changing character and truth, we are changed more into his likeness. As I wrote in *Pure Praise*, "We always become what we worship. If we focus on the world or other individuals, we'll become like them. If we focus on God, we'll become like him."[23]

When I think of remaining constant and consistent, I think of evangelist Luis Palau. He was known as "the Billy Graham of Latin America." He preached to millions in his crusades in many countries. I had the privilege of meeting Dr. Palau several years ago and eating dinner with him, along with several other young evangelists he was training and pouring into at the time. I recall being impressed with his humility and contagious smile. He was so full of joy and warmth. A few months ago I was invited to an online meeting where Dr. Palau spoke, and he was still doing what he did years ago: pouring into young ministers. I was mesmerized watching him speak that day. Some 25 years later, he was still full of joy and passion for the Lord. Only this time, he was suffering from terminal lung cancer. Yet even in his pain and close to death, he was still constant "in season and out of season." What a huge heart for worship!

Crucified

In verse 17 of Psalm 51 David prays, "The way to please you is to be truly sorry deep in our hearts. This is the kind of sacrifice you won't refuse" (CEV). David was sincerely broken in pieces over his sin. As Matthew Henry writes, his was "a heart that is tender, and pliable to God's word. Oh that there were such a heart in every one of us!"[24]

The only way you and I can have such a heart as David's is to die to ourselves. Our old heart and nature can't worship God in spirit and truth. That is why our old heart must be crucified.

🎵 Read Galatians 2:20. What do you think Paul meant when he said he was "crucified with Christ"?

In his book, *The Normal Christian Life*, Watchman Nee describes the moment when he realized his oneness with Christ's death. He said, "I was upstairs sitting at my desk reading the Word and praying, and I said, 'Lord, open my eyes!' And then in a flash I saw it…I saw that I was in him, and that when he died, I died…I was carried away with such joy at this great discovery that I jumped from my chair and cried, 'Praise the Lord, I am dead!' I ran downstairs and met one of the brothers helping in the kitchen and laid hold of him. 'Brother,' I said, 'do you know that I have died?' I must admit he looked puzzled. 'What do you mean?' he said, so I went on: 'Do you know that Christ has died? Do you know that I died with him? Do you know that my death is no less a fact that his?' Oh, it was so real to me! I longed to go through the streets of Shanghai shouting the news of my discovery. From that day to this I have never for one moment doubted the finality of that word: 'I have been crucified with Christ.'"[25]

Courageous

David followed up his prayer for a broken heart with an unexpected request: "May it please you to prosper Zion, to build up the walls of Jerusalem" (verse 18). It may seem abrupt that he would suddenly shift gears and change subjects like that. But he had prayed for his own self, and now, in classic worshiper fashion, he immediately turned his sights to others he was concerned for. Scholars say he may have been talking about literal walls he was already working on to protect the city of Jerusalem.[26] One thing is for sure: he was thinking beyond himself.

David was apparently petitioning God to allow him to continue his work. That's pretty bold, considering what he had just confessed. But worshipers know their sins are forgiven, because they know their God. David had confidence in God's everlasting mercy and in his relationship with the Lord. That gave him great courage to move forward with God's strength and blessing, to finish the work the Lord had called him to do. The mark of a true worshiper is their fortitude to step out and do what few would do.

We have many courageous Christians who serve as NLW team members around the world, including some who worship God in dangerous places. Take Mark and his dad, for example. Every week they go out and share Christ with Muslim and Hindu people living in tents in the slum areas of Pakistan. They bring them food and a give them a Bible. Then they tell them of the hope they have in Jesus Christ. Mark and his dad love worshiping God, and as part of our team at NLW International, they are teaching many others to worship him as well.

Matter of the Will

Samuel said to King Saul, "Your kingdom will not endure; the Lord has sought out a man after his own heart and appointed him ruler of his people, because you have not kept the Lord's command" (1 Samuel 13:14). David was the man God had appointed. But Samuel wasn't referring to David's heart. Notice it says God sought someone after *his* own heart–the Lord's heart. God wanted one who would fulfill all the desires of *his* heart and not oppose them. He knew David would do that. David had a proven track record of desiring God and choosing to worship him.

What I want us to see is that David didn't just naturally worship God because he had a special heart for God. Samuel called him a *man*, a human being like the rest of us. In his prayer David said, "Surely I was sinful at birth, sinful from the time my mother conceived me" (Psalm 51:5). David didn't come into the world and immediately start worshiping. It was a choice he had to make. In Psalm 63:8 David writes, "My soul clings to you." The King James translates it as "My soul follows hard after you." The word there for *soul* means the mind, will, and emotions. He made a choice in his mind to follow God. He was a man after God's heart, but that did not mean his worship came naturally for him. He chose to follow hard after God. He *chose* to worship.

To say someone has a heart for worship doesn't mean that person has a natural inclination toward it, as though they have mindlessly worshiped God from birth. It's just the opposite, in fact. All of us were born into sin. Our natural inclination is toward rebellion and evil, not toward worship. But if we know Christ as Savior, then God has put a new heart and his Spirit within us. So, every day we must die to ourselves and allow the Holy Spirit to reign inside of us. Only then can we rise above our natural bent toward evil and choose to worship our most awesome and worthy Lord.

Living the Prayer

2 Chronicles 16:9a says, "The eyes of the LORD search the whole earth in order to strengthen those whose hearts are fully committed to him" (NLT). The Lord notices if you are worshiping and earnestly seeking him. Like Mark and his dad in Pakistan, God sees you and supports you. Simply walk his trail and trust him to guide you, provide for you and connect you with those he wants you to know. Continue to faithfully pray the prayer model each day. As you do, be assured you have God's attention, because your heart for worship is completely his.

169

As we close our study together invest some time on your knees praying for the Lord's will to be done in your life. Thank him for all he has taught you these past weeks. Allow this time to be a powerful and galvanizing experience of worship that you won't soon forget. End by quoting the Lord's Prayer aloud with confidence, conviction and fervor!

JOURNAL

WEEK 5 FOLLOW-UP QUESTIONS FOR GROUP DISCUSSION

1. Share with the group your translation of John 15: 1-17. What is the gist of it? What does it mean to you?

2. Just before the "Praying the Prayer" section in Day 1 is the statement "Interceding for [others] can become a catalyst the Holy Spirit uses to move us to action." What does this sentence mean?

3. Day 1 says, "The Lord's Prayer is a prayer of the heart for the heart." Explain that statement. Do you agree? Why or why not?

4. Think of a crisis situation you have experienced. Did your response include the steps given in the checklist in Day 2 that is based on the Model Prayer? If yes, how do you think responding in that way impacted the experience or even the outcome of the situation? If your answer is no, how might a response like the one outlined in the checklist have impacted the experience or outcome?

5. In Day 3, which of the "Tips to Decrease the Noise of Social Media" would be most difficult for you to follow? Why? Which are you willing to try?

6. Which of the sisters described in Luke 10:38-42 do you most identify with, Martha or Mary? Why?

7. John 15:7 talks about abiding in Jesus. Explain what you think that means.

8. Which of the benefits of intimate communion with God in Day 4 do you think is most important? Why?

9. Discuss what you think Paul meant in Galatians 2:20 when he said he had been "crucified with Christ."

10. Day 5 poses a hypothetical question: "What if God didn't continue to bless us?" What would your response be if this were to happen? Would it affect your prayer life?

11. What did Paul mean when he said that we are to present ourselves as a "living sacrifice" to God (Romans 12:1)? How does making that gesture affect our prayer lives?

12. Has the prayer pattern suggested by this book helped strengthen your prayer life? If so, how?

Footnotes for Week 5:

[1] James Clear, *Atomic Habits: An Easy & Proven Way to Build Good Habits & Break Bad Ones* (New York: Penguin Random House, 2018), 32.

[2] Charles Duhigg, *The Power of Habit: Why We Do What We Do in Life and Business* (New York: Penguin Random House, 2012), 19.

[3] *ibid.* p. 36

[4] Gill's Exposition of the Entire Bible, "Psalm 27," *Bible Hub,* https://biblehub.com/commentaries/gill/psalms/27.htm

[5] John Eldridge, Moving Mountains (Nashville: Nelson Books, 2016), 81.

[6] "Cacophony," *Dictionary.com,* https://www.dictionary.com/browse/cacophony.

[7] Vincent Kartheiser, "The Social Dilemma," Jeff Orlowski, 2020, Silicon Valley, CA, Exposure Labs, Netflix.

[8] Michael Gryboski, "Google searches for prayer 'skyrocket' amid coronavirus outbreak: report," *The Christian Post,* March 31, 2020, https://www.christianpost.com/us/google-searches-for-prayer-have-skyrocketed-amid-coronavirus-outbreak-report.html

[9] A.W. Tozer, *Prayer: Communing with God in Everything — Collected Insights from A.W. Tozer* (Moody: Chicago 2016), 152.

[10] *ibid,* p. 137.

[11] *ibid,* p. 41.

12 Marie Barnett, *Breathe,* Mercy/Vineyard Publishing (ASCAP), admin. in North America by Music Services o/b/o Vineyard Music USA, 1995.

[13] Dictionary.com, *"Commune,"* https://www.dictionary.com/browse/commune.

[14] Adrian Rogers, *When We Say Father: Unlocking the Power of the Lord's Prayer* (Nashville: B&H Publishing Group, 2108), chapter 1 (e-book).

15 Strong's Concordance, "3306. menó," *Bible Hub,* https://biblehub.com/greek/3306.htm.

16 "The Five Levels of Communication," *Habits for Well Being,* https://www.habitsforwellbeing.com/five-levels-communication.

[17] *ibid.*

[18] Marshall Davis, *The Practice of the Presence of God: In Modern English, Brother Lawrence,* 2013, Second Conversation.

[19] Matthew 6 Bible Commentary, "John Wesley's Explanatory Notes," *Christianity.com,* https://www.christianity.com/bible/commentary.php?com=wes&b=40&c=6.

2[0] C.H. Spurgeon, *The Treasury of David* (Grand Rapids, Michigan: Kregel Publications, 1976), 237

[21] *ibid.*

[22] Strong's Concordance, "Psalm 51:10," *Bible Hub,* https://biblehub.com/strongs/psalms/51-10.htm

[23] Dwayne Moore, *Pure Praise: A Heart-focused Bible Study on Worship* (Colorado Springs, Colorado: Group Publishing, 2008), 52

[24] Matthew Henry's Concise Commentary, "Psalm 51:17," *Bible Hub,* https://biblehub.com/commentaries/psalms/51-17.htm

[25] Watchman Nee, *The Normal Christian Life* (Wheaton, Illinois: Tyndale House, 1982), 64, 65.

[26] Barnes' Notes on the Bible, "Psalm 51:18," *Bible Hub,* https://biblehub.com/commentaries/psalms/51-18.htm